YOUR PERSONAL
HOROSCOPE
2017

♊

GEMINI

YOUR PERSONAL
HOROSCOPE
2017

GEMINI

22nd May–21st June

igloobooks

igloobooks

Published in 2016
by Igloo Books Ltd
Cottage Farm
Sywell
NN6 0BJ
www.igloobooks.com

FIR003 0716
2 4 6 8 10 9 7 5 3 1
ISBN: 978-1-78557-507-5

This is an abridged version of material originally published
in Old Moore's Horoscope and Astral Diary.

Cover images: iStock
Cover designed by Nicholas Gage

Printed and manufactured in China

CONTENTS

INTRODUCTION

Your Personal Horoscopes have been specifically created to allow you to get the most from astrological patterns and the way they have a bearing on not only your zodiac sign, but nuances within it. Using the diary section of the book you can read about the influences and possibilities of each and every day of the year. It will be possible for you to see when you are likely to be cheerful and happy or those times when your nature is in retreat and you will be more circumspect. The diary will help to give you a feel for the specific 'cycles' of astrology and the way they can subtly change your day-to-day life. For example, when you see the sign ☿, this means that the planet Mercury is retrograde at that time. Retrograde means it appears to be running backwards through the zodiac. Such a happening has a significant effect on communication skills, but this is only one small aspect of how the Personal Horoscope can help you.

With Your Personal Horoscope the story doesn't end with the diary pages. It includes simple ways for you to work out the zodiac sign the Moon occupied at the time of your birth, and what this means for your personality. In addition, if you know the time of day you were born, it is possible to discover your Ascendant, yet another important guide to your personal make-up and potential.

Many readers are interested in relationships and in knowing how well they get on with people of other astrological signs. You might also be interested in the way you appear to very different sorts of individuals. If you are such a person, the section on Venus will be of particular interest. Despite the rapidly changing position of this planet, you can work out your Venus sign, and learn what bearing it will have on your life.

Using Your Personal Horoscope you can travel on one of the most fascinating and rewarding journeys that anyone can take – the journey to a better realisation of self.

THE ESSENCE OF GEMINI

Exploring the Personality of Gemini the Twins

(22ND MAY–21ST JUNE)

What's in a sign?

When working at your best there isn't much doubt that you are one of the most popular people to be found anywhere in the zodiac. Why? Because you are bubbly, charming, full of fun and the perfect companion. But there's more to it than that. Your natural Mercurial charm could coax the birds down from the trees and you exude the sort of self-confidence that would convince almost anyone that you know exactly what you want, and how to go about getting it. Virtually any task you choose to undertake is done in a flash and when at your best you can remove more obstacles than a bulldozer.

So, you ask, if all this is true, why aren't I doing even better in life than I am? The simple fact is that beneath all the bravado and that oh-so-confident exterior is a small child, who is often lost and afraid in a world that can be complicated, large and threatening. If ever there was a person who epitomised a split personality, it surely has to be the typical Gemini subject. That impulsive, driving, Mercury-ruled enthusiasm simply insists on pushing you to the front of any queue, but once you are there the expectations of all those standing behind can begin to prey on your mind. This is why so many of your plans stall before they are brought to completion, and it also explains all those times that you simply run out of energy and virtually collapse into a heap. There is a lot to learn if you want to get the best out of what the zodiac has given you. Fortunately, life itself is your schoolyard and there is plenty you can do to make the very best of your natural talents.

Read through the following sections carefully, and when you have done so, get ready to put all your latent talents to the test. As you grow in confidence, so you will find that you are not as alone as you sometimes think. The keywords for the sign of Gemini are

9

'I think', but for you this isn't an insular process. Life itself is your launching pad to success and happiness – just as long as you learn to concentrate on the task at hand.

Gemini resources

The part of the zodiac occupied by the sign of Gemini, has, for many centuries, been recognised as the home of communication. Almost everything that you are as an individual is associated with your need to keep in constant touch with the world at large. This trait is so marked that Geminis seem to dream more than most other people, so that even in your sleep the need to keep looking, talking and explaining is as essential to you as breathing.

What might be slightly less well understood regarding the sign of the Twins is that you are a natural listener too. One of the reasons for your popularity is that you always seem interested in what those around you have to say. And beneath this desire to know is a latent ability to understand so much about your friends and relatives at an almost instinctive level. Gemini individuals can keep moving forward, even against heavy odds, just as long as a particular project or task feels right, and you should never underestimate the power of your instincts.

The level of your energy, and the way you project it into everything you do, can be inclined to leave others breathless. This is one of your secrets of success because you can be at the winning post so often, whilst others are still putting on their shoes. You are not a trend follower but rather a trendsetter, and no matter if you are on the dance floor of a trendy club, or on a senior citizens' trip to the coast, you are likely to be the centre of attention. The enterprising, interesting Gemini individual skips through life like a barefoot child and elicits just as much joy from those who stand and watch.

Beneath the happy-go-lucky exterior is a great deal more savvy than many astrologers were once willing to grant to the sign of the Twins. However, the advent of the multimedia age has brought Gemini to a society that it not only understands, but in which it excels. On the telephone, the computer and especially the World Wide Web, you spread your sense of fun and offer everyone you meet an invigorating dose of your enthusiasm, knowledge and zest for life.

Beneath the surface

It is likely that most Gemini individuals would consider themselves to be uncomplicated and easy to understand. 'What you see is what you get' seems to be a statement made extremely often by those born under this zodiac sign. It isn't at all true. On the contrary, the Gemini nature is multi-faceted, cranky and often obscure. In short, you have more skins than a Spanish onion. If Geminis have often been referred to as 'superficial' or 'shallow' they probably only have themselves to blame, since they are the first to describe themselves this way. But the truth is that you are a deep thinker – in fact one of the deepest of all. The only reason you don't consider yourself in this light is that your thought processes, like your speech, are lightning fast.

Because of its chatterbox ways, Gemini is often a very misunderstood zodiac sign. But listen to yourself talking. Many of the statements you make to those around you will be ended in questions such as 'Don't you think?'. Why should this be so? Well the fact is that you are never so certain of yourself as you want to give the impression of being, and as a result you invariably seek the confirmation of the world at large that your ideas and plans are sound. If the response you want is late, or not forthcoming at all, you tend to feel insecure and start to fidget. In time this leads to worrying, the worst possible state for the Gemini mind. The dividing line between mental and physical is not at all well defined in your case, so you will often seem most fatigued at those times when you are less than sure of your direction in life.

You almost always start out with the right intentions and would never deliberately hurt another individual. To your very core you are generous and kind. Unfortunately in a busy schedule there isn't always time to let your sensitivity show, and especially not when you live your life constantly in the fast lane. It is almost instinctive for Geminis to divide their lives into 'the job I am doing now', 'the task I will be undertaking in a few minutes' and 'the things I am planning for later'. But even your mind is only capable of so much, so it's essential that you find moments to stop the whirl and buzz of your innermost thoughts. To do so is the hardest task you will undertake, but it's the surest path to health and success that you can ever choose.

Making the best of yourself

It is quite clear that you were never cut out to be a monk or a nun, or at least not of the contemplative sort. Mental desert islands are a natural torture chamber to your zodiac sign and so it's obvious, right from the start, that you need other people just as much as plants need rain. On the other hand, you also need to stop thinking that you can be in control of everything. The hardest lesson for any Gemini to learn is to be selective. Gemini sees life like a wonderfully prepared buffet at which every successive dish offers something absolutely delicious. The idea of trying some of the treats later simply doesn't occur and at the level of daily life the result can often be mental indigestion. Concentration is the key, though without losing the essential freshness and appeal that is the hallmark of your natural personality. 'One job at once' is the best adage, but it doesn't come easy for you.

Your natural talents are suited to intellectual browsing, so you are definitely at your best where flexibility is present. The chances are that you don't really enjoy getting your hands dirty, but even this doesn't really matter as long as you are learning something on the way. You revel in absorbing responsibility and tend to think on your feet. Travel is important to you, not only because it broadens your mind, but also because you are naturally good at languages. You possess a very human touch; you are not frightened to show your emotions and work well alongside others. However, you might function even better if you maintained confidence in your decisions and tried rather less than you sometimes do to be popular with everyone. This comes easier when you are dealing with subject matter that you understand fully, and that in turn takes concentration, which you can only cultivate with practice.

The impressions you give

This section may appeal the most to Gemini subjects because you care deeply about the opinions others have of you. To a certain extent everything you do in a public sense is a sort of performance and just like an actor, you are interested in what the critics have to say. To a great extent you can relax, because there's a good chance that you are much loved. How could it be otherwise? You spread sunshine wherever you go, though it has to be said that you can promote a good deal of confusion too on occasions.

You have to be prepared to take on board the fact that some people will like you more than others do. This is a natural consequence of being such an upfront person. There are people who swim around in the sea of life without making so much as a ripple, but you are definitely not one of them. Some of the individuals you meet will simply not be turned on by the gregarious, enthusiastic, go-getting creature that you are. Once you understand this fact, and stop trying to force your attentions in the wrong direction, your life will be happier as a result.

Another way that you can help yourself is to cultivate humility. Gemini people know at least something about almost everything but there is truth in the adage that 'a little knowledge can be a dangerous thing'. The most successful of those born under the sign of the Twins have learned to defer to experts, most of whom don't take kindly to criticism. You can still maintain your own opinions, but a quiet self-assurance will win you more friends than forcing half-formed opinions on the world at large. On the whole though, you can relax because you are almost certainly more popular than you think you are.

The way forward

Age matters less to Gemini than it does to any other zodiac sign. The fact is that you are always young in your head, no matter how much some of your joints might creak. But even in a physical sense it is important to look after yourself and to recognise those areas that need the most attention. Gemini rules the chest, and especially the lungs, so you should never be a smoker. The sign is also related to the general nervous system, which is almost always pushed to the edge in your frantic attempts to get just as much out of life as possible. Relaxation is just as important as physical exercise, and since you naturally love words, reading is as good as anything. All the same, you shouldn't be constantly trying to learn something, and need to understand that entertainment for its own sake is often enough.

No matter how much your mind wanders, you need to be master of at least one subject – this is the way to success in a professional sense. Whatever your job (and Gemini people are rarely out of work) you will nearly always find yourself in charge of others. Use all the natural understanding that lies at the centre of your being to understand how others tick and you are almost certain to prosper.

On the way through life, professional or social, you can't avoid dealing in gossip, because this is an essential part of the way you function. Casual contacts are inevitable, so you may have hundreds of acquaintances but only a few very close personal friends. However, when you do find yourself absolutely on the same wavelength as another individual, it can be the most enlightening experience imaginable. Geminis often find themselves involved in more than one deep, romantic attachment in their lives, though this is far less likely if your partner is also your best friend.

Don't give in to self-doubt, but at the same time avoid like the plague giving the impression that you know everything. Cultivate patience and spend at least a few minutes each day doing absolutely nothing. Overall, balance is essential, and that isn't always easy to achieve when tottering along the tightrope of life. All the same, a Gemini who is at ease with him- or herself excels socially and grows wiser with every passing day.

GEMINI ON THE CUSP

Astrological profiles are altered for those people born at either the beginning or the end of a zodiac sign, or, more properly, on the cusps of a sign. In the case of Gemini this would be on the 22nd of May and for two or three days after, and similarly at the end of the sign, probably from the 19th to the 21st of June.

The Taurus Cusp – 22nd to 25th May

It would be fair to suggest that Gemini tends to predominate over almost any zodiac sign with which it is associated so that the trends of this most capricious and gregarious sign tend to show out well at both cusps. Heavily affected by Taurus, however, you are likely to be steadier and more willing to take your time over important matters. Staying power is better and the Taurean cusp inspires a quiet confidence on occasions that seems to contrast sharply with the more chatty qualities of the Twins. Entrenched attitudes are certainly more likely, with a need to prove a point and to seek objectives through determined effort. Taurus here does little to stem the generally cheerful qualities of Gemini but there is likely to be a more serious side to the nature and a willingness to exhibit the sort of patience that is often lacking in the Sun sign of Gemini.

In matters of love, you are more likely than most Geminis to show a high degree of constancy, even if settling on a partner is a longer process in your case. You can't be detached from relationships in the way that the dyed-in-the-wool Gemini can and it's important for you to know that you are loved. Professionally speaking, you have much going for you because in addition to the 'get ahead at any cost' quality that comes from the direction of the Twins, you are persevering, honourable, steadfast and reliable. It is probably in matters of business that the most positive qualities of this astrological matching are to be seen.

Health matters are also stabilised to a great extent on this cusp, partly because the nature is not half as nervy, and more care is taken to get the level of rest and relaxation that is just as important to Gemini. Less rush and push is evident, though a need for change and diversity probably won't be eradicated from your basic nature. There is a good chance that you are something of a home bird, at least most of the time, and family matters are often paramount in your mind. Probably the most noticeable trait is your tendency to be more tidy than the orthodox Gemini – which some would say is no bad thing.

The Cancer Cusp – 19th to 21st June

It could be that the gradual slip from the sign of Gemini to that of Cancer is slightly less well defined than is the case for Taurus and Gemini. However, when working as stereotypes Gemini and Cancer are radically different sorts of signs. Gemini seeks to intellectualise everything, so its catch phrase is 'I think', while Cancer's is 'I feel'. What we would therefore expect, in this case, is a gradually quieter and less fickle nature as the Sun climbs closer to Cancer. You are likely to show more genuine consideration for other people. Actually this is something of a misnomer because Gemini people are very caring too, it's simply a matter of you showing the tendency more, and you are certainly more tied to home and family than any true Gemini would be. A quiet perseverance typifies your individual nature and you are quite prepared to wait for your objectives to mature, which the Twins are less likely to do. Comfort and security are important to you, though, apparently paradoxically, you are a great traveller and love to see fresh fields and pastures new. Given the opportunity you could even find yourself living in some far, distant land.

In affairs of the heart, you are clearly more steadfast than Gemini and love to be loved. The difference here is that Gemini wants to be liked by everyone, but will quickly move on in cases where this proves to be difficult. You, on the other hand, would take any sort of rebuff as a personal insult and would work hard to reverse the situation. Confidence may not be your middle name, but you are supported by the Gemini ability to bluff your way through when necessary, even if the motivation involved is of a more consistent nature.

You may well be a person who has to rest in order to recharge batteries that sometimes run quite low. Your nervous system may not be all that strong on occasions and this fact could manifest itself in the form of stomach troubles of one sort or another. Common sense counts when it comes to looking after yourself and that's something that the sign of Cancer does possess. Whether you are often truly satisfied with yourself and your own efforts may sometimes be in doubt.

GEMINI AND ITS ASCENDANTS

The nature of every individual on the planet is composed of the rich variety of zodiac signs and planetary positions that were present at the time of their birth. Your Sun sign, which in your case is Gemini, is one of the many factors when it comes to assessing the unique person you are. Probably the most important consideration, other than your Sun sign, is to establish the zodiac sign that was rising over the eastern horizon at the time that you were born. This is your Ascending or Rising sign. Most popular astrology fails to take account of the Ascendant, and yet its importance remains with you from the very moment of your birth, through every day of your life. The Ascendant is evident in the way you approach the world, and so, when meeting a person for the first time, it is this astrological influence that you are most likely to notice first. Our Ascending sign essentially represents what we appear to be, while the Sun sign is what we feel inside ourselves.

The Ascendant also has the potential for modifying our overall nature. For example, if you were born at a time of day when Gemini was passing over the eastern horizon (this would be around the time of dawn) then you would be classed as a double Gemini. As such, you would typify this zodiac sign, both internally and in your dealings with others. However, if your Ascendant sign turned out to be a Water sign, such as Pisces, there would be a profound alteration of nature, away from the expected qualities of Gemini.

One of the reasons why popular astrology often ignores the Ascendant is that it has always been rather difficult to establish. We have found a way to make this possible by devising an easy-to-use table, which you will find on page 157 of this book. Using this, you can establish your Ascendant sign at a glance. You will need to know your rough time of birth, then it is simply a case of following the instructions.

For those readers who have no idea of their time of birth it might be worth allowing a good friend, or perhaps your partner, to read through the section that follows this introduction. Someone who deals with you on a regular basis may easily discover your Ascending sign, even though you could have some difficulty establishing it for yourself. A good understanding of this component of your nature is essential if you want to be aware of that 'other person' who is responsible for the way you make contact with the world at large. Your Sun sign, Ascendant sign, and the other pointers in this book will, together, allow you a far better understanding of what makes you tick as an individual. Peeling back the different layers of your astrological make-up can be an enlightening experience, and the Ascendant may represent one of the most important layers of all.

Gemini with Gemini Ascendant

You are one of the most fun-loving characters in the zodiac, with a great sense of humour and the ability to sell refrigerators to Eskimos. Most people would think that you have nerves of steel and that there is nothing that lies beyond the scope of your ready wit and silver tongue. Unfortunately it isn't quite as simple as this because you bruise easily, especially when you discover that someone is not as fond of you as they might be. Routines get on your nerves and you need as much change and diversity as life will allow. You are the life and soul of any party that is going on in your vicinity, and you have the ability to mix business and pleasure so should get on well as a result.

In love you tend to be rather fickle and the double Gemini is inclined to dodge from relationship to relationship in pursuit of something that remains rather difficult to define. There are occasions when your life lacks stability and this can be provided by the right sort of personal attachment, assuming you manage to find it eventually. It is clear that you are not the easiest person to understand, even though you probably think that you do not have a complicated bone in your body. Most important of all, you have many, many friends, and this will be the case all your life.

Gemini with Cancer Ascendant

Many astrologers would say that this is a happy combination because some of the more flighty qualities of Gemini are somewhat modified by the steady influence of Cancer the Crab. To all intents and purposes you show the friendly and gregarious qualities of Gemini, but there is a thoughtful and even sometimes a serious quality that would not be present in the double Gemini example above. Looking after people is high on your list of priorities and you do this most of the time. This is made possible because you have greater staying power than Gemini is usually said to possess and you can easily see fairly complicated situations through to their conclusion without becoming bored on the way.

The chances are that you will have many friends and that these people show great concern for your well-being, because you choose them carefully and show them a great deal of consideration. However, you will still be on the receiving end of gossip on occasions, and need to treat such situations with a healthy pinch of salt. Like all Geminis, your nervous system is not as strong as you would wish to believe and family pressures in particular can put great strain on you. Activities of all kinds take your fancy and many people with this combination are attracted to sailing or wind surfing.

Gemini with Leo Ascendant

Many Gemini people think about doing great things, whilst those who enjoy a Leo Ascendant do much more than simply think. You are the truly intrepid Gemini but you always keep a sense of humour and are especially good to be around. Bold and quite fearless, you are inclined to go where nobody has gone before, no matter if this is into a precarious business venture or up a mountain that has not been previously climbed. It is people such as you who first explored the world and you love to know what lies around the next corner and over the far hill.

Kind and loving, you are especially loyal to your friends and would do almost anything on their behalf. As a result they show the greatest concern for you too. However, there are times when the cat walks alone and you are probably better at being on your own than would often be the case for the typical Gemini subject. In many ways you are fairly self-contained and don't tend to get bored too much unless you are forced to do the same things time and time again. You have a great sense of fun, can talk to anyone and usually greet the world with a big smile.

Gemini with Virgo Ascendant

A Virgo Ascendant means that you are ruled by Mercury, both through your Sun sign and through the sign that was rising at the time of your birth. This means that words are your basic tools in life and you use them to the full. Some writers have this combination because even speaking to people virtually all the time is not enough. Although you have many friends, you are fairly high-minded which means that you can make enemies too. The fact is that people either care very much for you, or else they don't like you at all. This can be difficult for you to come to terms with because you don't really set out to cause friction – it often simply attracts itself to you.

Although you love to travel, home is important too. There is a basic insecurity in your nature that comes about as a result of an overdose of Mercury, which makes you nervy and sometimes far less confident than anyone would guess. Success in your life may be slower arriving with this combination because you are determined to achieve your objectives on your own terms and this can take time. Always a contradiction, often a puzzle to others, your ultimate happiness in life is directly proportional to the effort you put in, though this should not mean wearing yourself out on the way.

Gemini with Libra Ascendant

What a happy-go-lucky soul you are, and how popular you tend to be with those around you. Libra is, like Gemini, an Air sign and this means that you are the communicator par excellence, even by Gemini standards. It can sometimes be difficult for you to make up your mind about things because Libra does not exactly aid this process, and especially not when it is allied to Mercurial Gemini. Frequent periods of deep thought are necessary and meditation would do you a great deal of good. All the same, although you might sometimes be rather unsure of yourself, you are rarely without a certain balance. Clean and tidy surroundings suit you the best, though this is far from easy to achieve because you are invariably dashing off to some place or other, so you really need someone to sort things out in your absence.

The most important fact of all is that you are much loved by your friends, of which there are likely to be very many. Because you are so willing to help them out, in return they are usually there when it matters and they would probably go to almost any length on your behalf. You exhibit a fine sense of justice and will usually back those in trouble. Charities tend to be attractive to you and you do much on behalf of those who live on the fringes of society or people who are truly alone.

Gemini with Scorpio Ascendant

What you are and what you appear to be can be two entirely different things with this combination. Although you appear to be every bit as chatty and even as flighty as Gemini tends to be, nothing could be further from the truth. In reality you have many deep and penetrating insights, all of which are geared towards sorting out potential problems before they come along. Few people would have the ability to pull the wool over your eyes and you show a much more astute face to the world than is often the case for Gemini taken on its own. The level of your confidence, although not earth-shattering, is much greater with this combination, and you would not be thwarted once you had made up your mind.

There is a slight danger here however because Gemini is always inclined to nerve problems of one sort or another. In the main these are slight and fleeting, though the presence of Scorpio can intensify reactions and heighten the possibility of depression, which would not be at all fortunate. The best way round this potential problem is to have a wealth of friends, plenty to do and the sort of variety in your life that suits your Mercury ruler. Financial success is not too difficult to achieve with this combination, mainly because you can easily earn money and then have a natural ability to hold on to it.

Gemini with Sagittarius Ascendant

'Tomorrow is another day!' This is your belief and you stick to it. There isn't a brighter or more optimistic soul to be found than you and almost everyone you come into contact with is touched by the fact. Dashing about from one place to another, you manage to get more things done in one day than most other people would achieve in a week. Of course this explains why you are so likely to wear yourself out, and it means that frequent periods of absolute rest are necessary if you are to remain truly healthy and happy. Sagittarius makes you brave and sometimes a little headstrong, so you need to curb your natural enthusiasms now and again, whilst you stop to think about the consequences of some of your actions.

It's not really certain if you do 'think' in the accepted sense of the word, because the lightning qualities of both these signs mean that your reactions are second to none. However, you are not indestructible and you put far more pressure on yourself than would often be sensible. Routines are not your thing at all and many of you manage to hold down two or more jobs at once. It might be an idea to stop and smell the flowers on the way and you could certainly do with putting your feet up much more than you do. However, you probably won't even have read this far into the passage because you will almost certainly have something far more important to do!

Gemini with Capricorn Ascendant

A much more careful and considered combination is evident here. You still have the friendly and chatty qualities of Gemini, though you also possess an astute, clever and deep-thinking quality which can really add bite to the Mercurial aspects of your nature. Although you rarely seem to take yourself or anyone else all that seriously, in reality you are not easily fooled and usually know the direction in which you are heading. The practical application of your thought processes matter to you and you always give of your best, especially in any professional situation. This combination provides the very best business mind that any Gemini could have and, unlike other versions of the sign, you are willing to allow matters to mature. This quality cannot be overstated, and leads to a form of ultimate achievement that many other Geminis would only guess at.

Family matters are important to you and your home is a special place of retreat, even though you are also willing to get out and meet the world, which is the prerogative of all Gemini types. There are times when you genuinely wish to remain quiet, and when such times arise you may need to explain the situation to some of the bemused people surrounding you. Above all you look towards material gain, though without ever losing your sense of humour.

Gemini with Aquarius Ascendant

If you were around in the 1960s there is every chance that you were the first to go around with flowers in your hair. You are unconventional, original, quirky and entertaining. Few people would fail to notice your presence and you take life as it comes, even though on most occasions you are firmly in the driving seat. In all probability you care very much about the planet on which you live and the people with whom you share it. Not everyone understands you, but that does not really matter, for you have more than enough communication skills to put your message across intact. You should avoid wearing yourself out by worrying about things that you cannot control and you definitely gain from taking time out to meditate. However, whether or not you allow yourself that luxury remains to be seen.

If you are not the most communicative form of Gemini subject then you must come a close second. Despite this fact, much of what you have to say makes real sense and you revel in the company of interesting, intelligent and stimulating people, whose opinions on a host of matters will add to your own considerations. You are a true original in every sense of the word and the mere fact of your presence in the world is bound to add to the enjoyment of life experienced by the many people with whom you make contact in your daily life.

Gemini with Pisces Ascendant

There is great duality inherent with this combination, and sometimes this can cause a few problems. Part of the trouble stems from the fact that you often fail to realise what you want from life and you could also be accused of failing to take the time out to think things through carefully enough. You are reactive, and although you have every bit of the natural charm that typifies the sign of Gemini, you are more prone to periods of self-doubt and confusion. However, you should not allow these facts to get you down too much because you are also genuinely loved and have a tremendous capacity to look after others, a factor which is more important to you than any other. It's true that personal relationships can sometimes be a cause of difficulty for you, partly because your constant need to know what makes other people tick could drive them up the wall. Accepting people at face value seems to be the best key to happiness of a personal sort and there are occasions when your very real and natural intuition has to be put on hold.

It's likely that you are an original, particularly in the way you dress. An early rebellious stage often gives way to a more comfortable form of eccentricity. When you are at your best just about everyone adores you.

Gemini with Aries Ascendant

A fairly jolly combination this, though by no means easy for others to come to terms with. You fly about from pillar to post and rarely stop long enough to take a breath. Admittedly this suits your own needs very well, but it can be a source of some disquiet to those around you, since they may not possess your energy or motivation. Those who know you well are deeply in awe of your capacity to keep going long after almost everyone else would have given up and gone home, though this quality is not always wonderful, because it means that you put more pressure on your nervous system than just about any other astrological combination.

You need to be mindful of your nervous system, which responds to the erratic, Mercurial quality of Gemini. Problems only really arise when the Aries part of you makes demands that the Gemini component finds difficult to deal with. There are paradoxes galore here and some of them need sorting out if you are ever fully to understand yourself, or are to be in a position when others know what makes you tick.

In relationships you might be a little fickle, but you are a veritable charmer and never stuck for the right words, no matter who you are dealing with. Your tenacity knows no bounds, though perhaps it should!

Gemini with Taurus Ascendant

This is a generally happy combination which finds you better able to externalise the cultured and creative qualities that are inherent in your Taurean side. You love to be around interesting and stimulating people and tend to be just as talkative as the typical Gemini is expected to be. The reason why Gemini helps here is because it lightens the load somewhat. Taurus is not the most introspective sign of the zodiac, but it does have some of that quality, and a Gemini Sun allows you to speak your mind more freely and, as a result, to know yourself better too.

Although your mind tends to be fairly logical, you also enjoy flashes of insight that can cause you to behave in a less rational way from time to time. This is probably no bad thing because life will never be boring with you around. You try to convince yourself that you take on board all the many and varied opinions that come back at you from others, though there is a slight danger of intellectual snobbery if the responses you get are not the expected ones. You particularly like clean houses, funny people and probably fast cars. Financial rewards can come thick and fast to the Taurus-Ascendant Gemini when the logical but still inspirational mind is firmly harnessed to practical matters.

THE MOON AND THE PART IT PLAYS IN YOUR LIFE

In astrology the Moon is probably the single most important heavenly body after the Sun. Its unique position, as partner to the Earth on its journey around the solar system, means that the Moon appears to pass through the signs of the zodiac extremely quickly. The zodiac position of the Moon at the time of your birth plays a great part in personal character and is especially significant in the build-up of your emotional nature.

Your Own Moon Sign

Discovering the position of the Moon at the time of your birth has always been notoriously difficult because tracking the complex zodiac positions of the Moon is not easy. This process has been reduced to three simple stages with our Lunar Tables. A breakdown of the Moon's zodiac positions can be found from page 35 onwards, so that once you know what your Moon Sign is, you can see what part this plays in the overall build-up of your personal character.

If you follow the instructions on the next page you will soon be able to work out exactly what zodiac sign the Moon occupied on the day that you were born and you can then go on to compare the reading for this position with those of your Sun sign and your Ascendant. It is partly the comparison between these three important positions that goes towards making you the unique individual you are.

HOW TO DISCOVER YOUR MOON SIGN

This is a three-stage process. You may need a pen and a piece of paper but if you follow the instructions below the process should only take a minute or so.

STAGE 1 First of all you need to know the Moon Age at the time of your birth. If you look at Moon Table 1, on page 33, you will find all the years between 1919 and 2017 down the left side. Find the year of your birth and then trace across to the right to the month of your birth. Where the two intersect you will find a number. This is the date of the New Moon in the month that you were born. You now need to count forward the number of days between the New Moon and your own birthday. For example, if the New Moon in the month of your birth was shown as being the 6th and you were born on the 20th, your Moon Age Day would be 14. If the New Moon in the month of your birth came after your birthday, you need to count forward from the New Moon in the previous month. Whatever the result, jot this number down so that you do not forget it.

STAGE 2 Take a look at Moon Table 2 on page 34. Down the left hand column look for the date of your birth. Now trace across to the month of your birth. Where the two meet you will find a letter. Copy this letter down alongside your Moon Age Day.

STAGE 3 Moon Table 3 on page 34 will supply you with the zodiac sign the Moon occupied on the day of your birth. Look for your Moon Age Day down the left hand column and then for the letter you found in Stage 2. Where the two converge you will find a zodiac sign and this is the sign occupied by the Moon on the day that you were born.

Your Zodiac Moon Sign Explained

You will find a profile of all zodiac Moon Signs on pages 35 to 38, showing in yet another way how astrology helps to make you into the individual that you are. In each daily entry of the Astral Diary you can find the zodiac position of the Moon for every day of the year. This also allows you to discover your lunar birthdays. Since the Moon passes through all the signs of the zodiac in about a month, you can expect something like twelve lunar birthdays each year. At these times you are likely to be emotionally steady and able to make the sort of decisions that have real, lasting value.

MOON TABLE 1

YEAR	APR	MAY	JUN	YEAR	APR	MAY	JUN	YEAR	APR	MAY	JUN
1919	30	29	27	1952	24	23	22	1985	20	19	18
1920	18	18	16	1953	13	13	11	1986	9	8	7
1921	8	7	6	1954	3	2 1/30		1987	28	27	26
1922	27	26	25	1955	22	21	20	1988	16	15	14
1923	16	15	14	1956	11	10	8	1989	6	5	3
1924	4	3	2	1957	29	29	27	1990	25	24	22
1925	23	22	21	1958	19	18	17	1991	13	13	11
1926	12	11	10	1959	8	7	6	1992	3	2 1/30	
1927	2	1/30	29	1960	26	26	24	1993	22	21	20
1928	20	19	18	1961	15	14	13	1994	11	10	9
1929	9	9	7	1962	5	4	2	1995	30	29	27
1930	28	28	26	1963	23	23	21	1996	18	18	17
1931	18	17	16	1964	12	11	10	1997	7	6	5
1932	6	5	4	1965	1	1/30	29	1998	26	25	24
1933	24	24	23	1966	20	19	18	1999	16	15	13
1934	13	13	12	1967	9	8	7	2000	4	4	2
1935	3	2 1/30		1968	28	27	26	2001	23	23	21
1936	21	20	19	1969	16	15	14	2002	12	12	10
1937	12	10	8	1970	6	6	4	2003	1	1/30	29
1938	30	29	27	1971	25	24	22	2004	18	16	15
1939	19	19	17	1972	13	13	11	2005	8	8	6
1940	7	7	6	1973	3	2 1/30		2006	27	27	26
1941	26	26	24	1974	22	21	20	2007	17	171	15
1942	15	15	13	1975	11	11	9	2008	6	5	4
1943	4	4	2	1976	29	29	27	2009	26	25	23
1944	22	22	20	1977	18	18	16	2010	14	14	12
1945	12	11	10	1978	7	7	5	2011	3	3	2
1946	2	1/30	29	1979	26	26	24	2012	21	20	19
1947	20	19	18	1980	15	14	13	2013	10	10	8
1948	9	9	7	1981	4	4	2	2014	30	29	27
1949	28	27	26	1982	23	21	20	2015	19	18	17
1950	17	17	15	1983	13	12	11	2016	7	6	4
1951	6	6	4	1984	1	1/30	29	2017	25	25	24

TABLE 2   MOON TABLE 3

DAY	MAY	JUN	M/D	M	N	O	P	Q	R	S
1	M	O	0	TA	GE	GE	GE	CA	CA	CA
2	M	P	1	GE	GE	GE	CA	CA	CA	LE
3	M	P	2	GE	GE	CA	CA	CA	LE	LE
4	M	P	3	GE	CA	CA	CA	LE	LE	LE
5	M	P	4	CA	CA	CA	LE	LE	LE	VI
6	M	P	5	CA	LE	LE	LE	VI	VI	VI
7	M	P	6	LE	LE	LE	VI	VI	VI	LI
8	M	P	7	LE	LE	VI	VI	VI	LI	LI
9	M	P	8	LE	VI	VI	VI	LI	LI	LI
10	M	P	9	VI	VI	VI	LI	LI	SC	SC
11	M	P	10	VI	LI	LI	LI	SC	SC	SC
12	N	Q	11	LI	LI	SC	SC	SC	SA	SA
13	N	Q	12	LI	LI	SC	SC	SA	SA	SA
14	N	Q	13	LI	SC	SC	SC	SA	SA	SA
15	N	Q	14	LI	SC	SC	SA	SA	SA	CP
16	N	Q	15	SC	SA	SA	SA	CP	CP	CP
17	N	Q	16	SC	SA	SA	CP	CP	CP	AQ
18	N	Q	17	SA	SA	CP	CP	CP	AQ	AQ
19	N	Q	18	SA	CP	CP	CP	AQ	AQ	AQ
20	N	Q	19	SA	CP	CP	AQ	AQ	AQ	PI
21	N	Q	20	CP	AQ	AQ	AQ	PI	PI	PI
22	O	R	21	CP	AQ	AQ	PI	PI	PI	AR
23	O	R	22	AQ	AQ	PI	PI	PI	AR	AR
24	O	R	23	AQ	PI	PI	PI	AR	AR	AR
25	O	R	24	AQ	PI	PI	AR	AR	AR	TA
26	O	R	25	PI	AR	AR	AR	TA	TA	TA
27	O	R	26	PI	AR	AR	TA	TA	TA	GE
28	O	R	27	AR	AR	TA	TA	TA	GE	GE
29	O	R	28	AR	TA	TA	TA	GE	GE	GE
30	O	R	29	AR	TA	TA	GE	GE	GE	CA
31	O	–								

AR = Aries, TA = Taurus, GE = Gemini, CA = Cancer, LE = Leo, VI = Virgo,
LI = Libra, SC = Scorpio, SA = Sagittarius, CP = Capricorn, AQ = Aquarius, PI = Pisces

MOON SIGNS

Moon in Aries

You have a strong imagination, courage, determination and a desire to do things in your own way and forge your own path through life.

Originality is a key attribute; you are seldom stuck for ideas although your mind is changeable and you could take the time to focus on individual tasks. Often quick-tempered, you take orders from few people and live life at a fast pace. Avoid health problems by taking regular time out for rest and relaxation.

Emotionally, it is important that you talk to those you are closest to and work out your true feelings. Once you discover that people are there to help, there is less necessity for you to do everything yourself.

Moon in Taurus

The Moon in Taurus gives you a courteous and friendly manner, which means you are likely to have many friends.

The good things in life mean a lot to you, as Taurus is an Earth sign that delights in experiences which please the senses. Hence you are probably a lover of good food and drink, which may in turn mean you need to keep an eye on the bathroom scales, especially as looking good is also important to you.

Emotionally you are fairly stable and you stick by your own standards. Taureans do not respond well to change. Intuition also plays an important part in your life.

Moon in Gemini

You have a warm-hearted character, sympathetic and eager to help others. At times reserved, you can also be articulate and chatty: this is part of the paradox of Gemini, which always brings duplicity to the nature. You are interested in current affairs, have a good intellect, and are good company and likely to have many friends. Most of your friends have a high opinion of you and would be ready to defend you should the need arise. However, this is usually unnecessary, as you are quite capable of defending yourself in any verbal confrontation.

Travel is important to your inquisitive mind and you find intellectual stimulus in mixing with people from different cultures. You also gain much from reading, writing and the arts but you do need plenty of rest and relaxation in order to avoid fatigue.

Moon in Cancer

The Moon in Cancer at the time of birth is a fortunate position as Cancer is the Moon's natural home. This means that the qualities of compassion and understanding given by the Moon are especially enhanced in your nature, and you are friendly and sociable and cope well with emotional pressures. You cherish home and family life, and happily do the domestic tasks. Your surroundings are important to you and you hate squalor and filth. You are likely to have a love of music and poetry.

Your basic character, although at times changeable like the Moon itself, depends on symmetry. You aim to make your surroundings comfortable and harmonious, for yourself and those close to you.

Moon in Leo

The best qualities of the Moon and Leo come together to make you warm-hearted, fair, ambitious and self-confident. With good organisational abilities, you invariably rise to a position of responsibility in your chosen career. This is fortunate as you don't enjoy being an 'also-ran' and would rather be an important part of a small organisation than a menial in a large one.

You should be lucky in love, and happy, provided you put in the effort to make a comfortable home for yourself and those close to you. It is likely that you will have a love of pleasure, sport, music and literature. Life brings you many rewards, most of them as a direct result of your own efforts, although you may be luckier than average and ready to make the best of any situation.

Moon in Virgo

You are endowed with good mental abilities and a keen receptive memory, but you are never ostentatious or pretentious. Naturally quite reserved, you still have many friends, especially of the opposite sex. Marital relationships must be discussed carefully and worked at so that they remain harmonious, as personal attachments can be a problem if you do not give them your full attention.

Talented and persevering, you possess artistic qualities and are a good homemaker. Earning your honours through genuine merit, you work long and hard towards your objectives but show little pride in your achievements. Many short journeys will be undertaken in your life.

Moon in Libra

With the Moon in Libra you are naturally popular and make friends easily. People like you, probably more than you realise, you bring fun to a party and are a natural diplomat. For all its good points, Libra is not the most stable of astrological signs and, as a result, your emotions can be a little unstable too. Therefore, although the Moon in Libra is said to be good for love and marriage, your Sun sign and Rising sign will have an important effect on your emotional and loving qualities.

You must remember to relate to others in your decision-making. Co-operation is crucial because Libra represents the 'balance' of life that can only be achieved through harmonious relationships. Conformity is not easy for you because Libra, an Air sign, likes its independence.

Moon in Scorpio

Some people might call you pushy. In fact, all you really want to do is to live life to the full and protect yourself and your family from the pressures of life. Take care to avoid giving the impression of being sarcastic or impulsive and use your energies wisely and constructively.

You have great courage and you invariably achieve your goals by force of personality and sheer effort. You are fond of mystery and are good at predicting the outcome of situations and events. Travel experiences can be beneficial to you.

You may experience problems if you do not take time to examine your motives in a relationship, and also if you allow jealousy, always a feature of Scorpio, to cloud your judgement.

Moon in Sagittarius

The Moon in Sagittarius helps to make you a generous individual with humanitarian qualities and a kind heart. Restlessness may be intrinsic as your mind is seldom still. Perhaps because of this, you have a need for change that could lead you to several major moves during your adult life. You are not afraid to stand your ground when you know your judgement is right, you speak directly and have good intuition.

At work you are quick, efficient and versatile and so you make an ideal employee. You need work to be intellectually demanding and do not enjoy tedious routines.

In relationships, you anger quickly if faced with stupidity or deception, though you are just as quick to forgive and forget. Emotionally, there are times when your heart rules your head.

Moon in Capricorn

The Moon in Capricorn makes you popular and likely to come into the public eye in some way. The watery Moon is not entirely comfortable in the Earth sign of Capricorn and this may lead to some difficulties in the early years of life. An initial lack of creative ability and indecision must be overcome before the true qualities of patience and perseverance inherent in Capricorn can show through.

You have good administrative ability and are a capable worker, and if you are careful you can accumulate wealth. But you must be cautious and take professional advice in partnerships, as you are open to deception. You may be interested in social or welfare work, which suit your organisational skills and sympathy for others.

Moon in Aquarius

The Moon in Aquarius makes you an active and agreeable person with a friendly, easy-going nature. Sympathetic to the needs of others, you flourish in a laid-back atmosphere. You are broad-minded, fair and open to suggestion, although sometimes you have an unconventional quality which others can find hard to understand.

You are interested in the strange and curious, and in old articles and places. You enjoy trips to these places and gain much from them. Political, scientific and educational work interests you and you might choose a career in science or technology.

Money-wise, you make gains through innovation and concentration and Lunar Aquarians often tackle more than one job at a time. In love you are kind and honest.

Moon in Pisces

You have a kind, sympathetic nature, somewhat retiring at times, but you always take account of others' feelings and help when you can.

Personal relationships may be problematic, but as life goes on you can learn from your experiences and develop a better understanding of yourself and the world around you.

You have a fondness for travel, appreciate beauty and harmony and hate disorder and strife. You may be fond of literature and would make a good writer or speaker yourself. You have a creative imagination and may come across as an incurable romantic. You have strong intuition, maybe bordering on a mediumistic quality, which sets you apart from the mass. You may not be rich in cash terms, but your personal gifts are worth more than gold.

GEMINI IN LOVE

Discover how compatible in love you are with people from the same and other signs of the zodiac. Five stars equals a match made in heaven!

Gemini meets Gemini

Generally speaking, this match can be very successful because although Gemini people can be insecure, they basically feel they are quite 'together' sorts of people. Consequently, they experience a meeting of minds with fellow Twins. This relationship won't work at a distance, and depends on a degree of intimacy to negate the more flighty and showy qualities of the sign. Infidelity could be a potential problem, especially with two Gemini people in the picture, but jealousy doesn't usually prevail. Star rating: ****

Gemini meets Cancer

This is often a very good match. Cancer is a very caring sign and quite adaptable. Geminis are untidy, have butterfly minds and are usually full of a thousand different schemes which Cancerians take in their stride and even relish. They can often be the 'wind beneath the wings' of their Gemini partners. In return, Gemini can eradicate some of the Cancerian emotional insecurity and is more likely to be faithful in thought, word and deed to Cancer than to almost any other sign. Star rating: ****

Gemini meets Leo

There can be problems here, but Gemini is adaptable enough to overcome many of them. Leo is a go-getter and might sometimes rail against Gemini's flighty tendencies, while Gemini's mental disorganisation can undermine Leo's practicality. However, Leo is cheerful and enjoys Gemini's jokey, flippant qualities. At times of personal intimacy, the two signs should be compatible. Leo and Gemini share very high ideals, but Leo will stick at them for longer. Patience is needed on both sides for the relationship to develop. Star rating: ***

Gemini meets Virgo

The fact that both these signs are ruled by the planet Mercury might at first seem good but, unfortunately, Mercury works very differently in each of them. Gemini is untidy, flighty, quick, changeable and easily bored, while Virgo is fastidious, steady and constant. If Virgo is willing to accept some anarchy, all can be well, but this not usually the case. Virgoans are deep thinkers and may find Gemini a little superficial. This pair can be compatible intellectually, though even this side isn't without its problems. Star rating: ***

Gemini meets Libra

One of the best possible zodiac combinations. Libra and Gemini are both Air signs, which leads to a meeting of minds. Both signs simply love to have a good time, although Libra is the tidiest and less forgetful. Gemini's capricious nature won't bother Libra, who acts as a stabilising influence. Life should generally run smoothly, and any rows are likely to be short and sharp. Both parties genuinely like each other, which is of paramount importance in a relationship and, ultimately, there isn't a better reason for being or staying together. Star rating: *****

Gemini meets Scorpio

There could be problems here. Scorpio is one of the deepest and least understood of all the zodiac signs, which at first seems like a challenge to intellectual Gemini, who thinks it can solve anything. But the deeper the Gemini digs, the further down Scorpio goes. Meanwhile, Scorpio may be finding Gemini thoughtless, shallow and even downright annoying. Gemini is often afraid of Scorpio's strength, and the sting in its tail, both of which the perceptive Twins can instinctively recognise. Anything is possible, but the outlook for this match is less than promising. Star rating: **

Gemini meets Sagittarius

A paradoxical relationship this. On paper, the two signs have much
in common, but unfortunately, they are often so alike that life turns
into a fiercely fought competition. Both signs love change and
diversity and both want to be the life and soul of the party. But in life
there must always be a leader and a follower, and neither of this pair
wants to be second. Both also share a tendency towards infidelity,
which may develop into a problem as time passes. This could be an
interesting match, but not necessarily successful. Star rating: **

Gemini meets Capricorn

Gemini has a natural fondness for Capricorn, which at first may
be mutual. However, Capricorn is very organised, practical and
persevering, and always achieves its goals in the end. Gemini starts
out like this, but then changes direction on the way, using a more
instinctive and evolutionary approach than the Goat that may interfere
with the progress of mutual objectives. To compensate, Gemini helps
Capricorn to avoid taking itself too seriously, while Capricorn brings a
degree of stability into Gemini's world. When this pairing does work,
though, it will be spectacular! Star rating: ***

Gemini meets Aquarius

Aquarius is commonly mistaken for a Water sign, but in fact it's
ruled by the Air element, and this is the key to its compatibility with
Gemini. Both signs mix freely socially, and each has an insatiable
curiosity. There is plenty of action, lots of love but very little rest,
and so great potential for success if they don't wear each other out!
Aquarius revels in its own eccentricity, and encourages Gemini
to emulate this. Theirs will be an unconventional household, but
almost everyone warms to this crazy and unpredictable couple.
Star rating: *****

Gemini meets Pisces

Gemini likes to think of itself as intuitive and intellectual, and indeed sometimes it is, but it will never understand Pisces' dark depths. Another stumbling block is that both Gemini and Pisces are 'split' signs – the Twins and the two Fishes, which means that both are capable of dual personalities. There won't be any shortage of affection, but the real question has to be how much these people ultimately feel they have in common. Pisces is extremely kind, and so is Gemini most of the time. But Pisces does altogether too much soul-searching for Gemini, who might eventually become bored. Star rating: ***

Gemini meets Aries

Don't expect peace and harmony with this combination, although what comes along instead might make up for any disagreements. Gemini has a very fertile imagination, while Aries has the tenacity to make reality from fantasy. Combined, they have a sizzling relationship. There are times when it seems as though both parties will explode with indignation and something has to give. But even if there are clashes, making them up will always be most enjoyable! Mutual financial success is very likely in this match. Star rating: ****

Gemini meets Taurus

Gemini people can really infuriate the generally steady Taurean nature as they are so untidy, which is a complete reversal of the Taurean ethos. At first this won't matter; Mr or Miss Gemini is enchanting, entertaining and very different. But time will tell, and that's why this potential relationship only has two stars. There is some hope, however, because Taurus can curb some of the excesses of the Twins, whilst Gemini is more than capable of preventing the Bull from taking itself too seriously. Star rating: **

VENUS:
THE PLANET OF LOVE

If you look up at the sky around sunset or sunrise you will often see Venus in close attendance to the Sun. It is arguably one of the most beautiful sights of all and there is little wonder that historically it became associated with the goddess of love. But although Venus does play an important part in the way you view love and in the way others see you romantically, this is only one of the spheres of influence that it enjoys in your overall character.

Venus has a part to play in the more cultured side of your life and has much to do with your appreciation of art, literature, music and general creativity. Even the way you look is responsive to the part of the zodiac that Venus occupied at the start of your life, though this fact is also down to your Sun sign and Ascending sign. If, at the time you were born, Venus occupied one of the more gregarious zodiac signs, you will be more likely to wear your heart on your sleeve, as well as to be more attracted to entertainment, social gatherings and good company. If on the other hand Venus occupied a quiet zodiac sign at the time of your birth, you would tend to be more retiring and less willing to shine in public situations.

It's good to know what part the planet Venus plays in your life for it can have a great bearing on the way you appear to the rest of the world and since we all have to mix with others, you can learn to make the very best of what Venus has to offer you.

One of the great complications in the past has always been trying to establish exactly what zodiac position Venus enjoyed when you were born because the planet is notoriously difficult to track. However, we have solved that problem by creating a table that is exclusive to your Sun sign, which you will find on the following page.

Establishing your Venus sign could not be easier. Just look up the year of your birth on the following page and you will see a sign of the zodiac. This was the sign that Venus occupied in the period covered by your sign in that year. If Venus occupied more than one sign during the period, this is indicated by the date on which the sign changed, and the name of the new sign. For instance, if you were born in 1950, Venus was in Gemini until the 8th June, after which time it was in Cancer. If you were born before 8th June your Venus sign is Gemini, if you were born on or after 8th June, your Venus sign is Cancer. Once you have established the position of Venus at the time of your birth, you can then look in the pages which follow to see how this has a bearing on your life as a whole.

1919 CANCER / 8.6 LEO
1920 TAURUS / 3.6 GEMINI
1921 ARIES / 3.6 TAURUS
1922 GEMINI / 26.5 CANCER /
    21.6 LEO
1923 TAURUS / 15.6 GEMINI
1924 CANCER
1925 GEMINI / 9.6 CANCER
1926 ARIES / 2.6 TAURUS
1927 CANCER / 8.6 LEO
1928 TAURUS / 30.5 GEMINI
1929 ARIES / 4.6 TAURUS
1930 GEMINI / 22.5 CANCER /
    21.6 LEO
1931 TAURUS / 15.6 GEMINI
1932 CANCER
1933 GEMINI / 9.6 CANCER
1934 ARIES / 2.6 TAURUS
1935 CANCER / 8.6 LEO
1936 TAURUS / 30.5 GEMINI
1937 ARIES / 4.6 TAURUS
1938 GEMINI / 25.5 CANCER /
    20.6 LEO
1939 TAURUS / 14.6 GEMINI
1940 CANCER
1941 CANCER / 7.6 LEO
1942 GEMINI / 8.6 CANCER
1943 ARIES / 1.6 TAURUS
1944 CANCER / 7.6 LEO
1945 TAURUS / 29.5 GEMINI
1946 ARIES / 5.6 TAURUS
1947 GEMINI / 24.5 CANCER /
    19.6 LEO
1948 TAURUS / 14.6 GEMINI
1949 CANCER
1950 GEMINI / 8.6 CANCER
1951 ARIES / 1.6 TAURUS
1952 TAURUS / 29.5 GEMINI
1953 ARIES / 5.6 TAURUS
1954 GEMINI / 24.5 CANCER /
    19.6 LEO
1955 TAURUS / 13.6 GEMINI
1956 CANCER
1957 GEMINI / 7.6 CANCER
1958 ARIES / 31.5 TAURUS
1959 CANCER / 7.6 LEO
1960 TAURUS / 28.5 GEMINI
1961 ARIES / 6.6 TAURUS
1962 GEMINI / 24.5 CANCER /
    18.6 LEO
1963 TAURUS / 13.6 GEMINI
1964 CANCER / 17.6 GEMINI
1965 GEMINI / 7.6 CANCER
1966 ARIES / 31.5 TAURUS
1967 CANCER / 7.6 LEO
1968 TAURUS / 28.5 GEMINI
1969 ARIES / 6.6 TAURUS
1970 GEMINI / 23.5 CANCER /
    18.5 LEO

1971 TAURUS / 12.6 GEMINI
1972 CANCER / 12.6 GEMINI
1973 GEMINI / 6.6 CANCER
1974 ARIES / 30.5 TAURUS
1975 CANCER / 7.6 LEO
1976 TAURUS / 27.5 GEMINI
1977 ARIES / 7.6 TAURUS
1978 GEMINI / 23.5 CANCER /
    17.5 LEO
1979 TAURUS / 12.6 GEMINI
1980 CANCER / 6.6 GEMINI
1981 GEMINI / 6.6 CANCER
1982 ARIES / 30.5 TAURUS
1983 CANCER / 6.6 LEO
1984 TAURUS / 27.5 GEMINI /
    21.6 CANCER
1985 ARIES / 7.6 TAURUS
1986 GEMINI / 22.5 CANCER /
    17.5 LEO
1987 TAURUS / 11.6 GEMINI
1988 CANCER / 27.5 GEMINI
1989 GEMINI / 5.6 CANCER
1990 ARIES / 29.5 TAURUS
1991 CANCER / 6.6 LEO
1992 TAURUS / 26.5 GEMINI /
    20.6 CANCER
1993 ARIES / 7.6 TAURUS
1994 CANCER / 16.6 LEO
1995 TAURUS / 11.6 GEMINI
1996 CANCER / 27.5 GEMINI
1997 GEMINI / 4.6 CANCER
1998 ARIES / 29.5 TAURUS
1999 CANCER / 6.6 LEO
2000 TAURUS / 25.5 GEMINI /
    19.6 CANCER
2001 ARIES / 7.6 TAURUS
2002 CANCER / 15.6 LEO
2003 TAURUS / 11.6 GEMINI
2004 CANCER / 27.5 GEMINI
2005 GEMINI / 2.6 CANCER
2006 ARIES / 29.6 TAURUS
2007 CANCER / 6.6 LEO
2008 TAURUS / 25.5 GEMINI /
    19.6 CANCER
2009 ARIES / 7.6 TAURUS
2010 CANCER / 15.6 LEO
2011 TAURUS / 11.6 GEMINI
2012 CANCER / 27.5 GEMINI
2013 GEMINI / 2.6 CANCER
2014 ARIES / 29.6 TAURUS
2015 CANCER / 6.6 LEO
2016 GEMINI / 18.6 CANCER
2017 GEMINI / 7.6 CANCER

VENUS THROUGH THE ZODIAC SIGNS

Venus in Aries

Amongst other things, the position of Venus in Aries indicates a fondness for travel, music and all creative pursuits. Your nature tends to be affectionate and you would try not to create confusion or difficulty for others if it could be avoided. Many people with this planetary position have a great love of the theatre, and mental stimulation is of the greatest importance. Early romantic attachments are common with Venus in Aries, so it is very important to establish a genuine sense of romantic continuity. Early marriage is not recommended, especially if it is based on sympathy. You may give your heart a little too readily on occasions.

Venus in Taurus

You are capable of very deep feelings and your emotions tend to last for a very long time. This makes you a trusting partner and lover, whose constancy is second to none. In life you are precise and careful and always try to do things the right way. Although this means an ordered life, which you are comfortable with, it can also lead you to be rather too fussy for your own good. Despite your pleasant nature, you are very fixed in your opinions and quite able to speak your mind. Others are attracted to you and historical astrologers always quoted this position of Venus as being very fortunate in terms of marriage. However, if you find yourself involved in a failed relationship, it could take you a long time to trust again.

Venus in Gemini

As with all associations related to Gemini, you tend to be quite versatile, anxious for change and intelligent in your dealings with the world at large. You may gain money from more than one source but you are equally good at spending it. There is an inference here that you are a good communicator, via either the written or the spoken word, and you love to be in the company of interesting people. Always on the look-out for culture, you may also be very fond of music, and love to indulge the curious and cultured side of your nature. In romance you tend to have more than one relationship and could find yourself associated with someone who has previously been a friend or even a distant relative.

Venus in Cancer

You often stay close to home because you are very fond of family and enjoy many of your most treasured moments when you are with those you love. Being naturally sympathetic, you will always do anything you can to support those around you, even people you hardly know at all. This charitable side of your nature is your most noticeable trait and is one of the reasons why others are naturally so fond of you. Being receptive and in some cases even psychic, you can see through to the soul of most of those with whom you come into contact. You may not commence too many romantic attachments but when you do give your heart, it tends to be unconditionally.

Venus in Leo

It must become quickly obvious to almost anyone you meet that you are kind, sympathetic and yet determined enough to stand up for anyone or anything that is truly important to you. Bright and sunny, you warm the world with your natural enthusiasm and would rarely do anything to hurt those around you, or at least not intentionally. In romance you are ardent and sincere, though some may find your style just a little overpowering. Gains come through your contacts with other people and this could be especially true with regard to romance, for love and money often come hand in hand for those who were born with Venus in Leo. People claim to understand you, though you are more complex than you seem.

Venus in Virgo

Your nature could well be fairly quiet no matter what your Sun sign might be, though this fact often manifests itself as an inner peace and would not prevent you from being basically sociable. Some delays and even the odd disappointment in love cannot be ruled out with this planetary position, though it's a fact that you will usually find the happiness you look for in the end. Catapulting yourself into romantic entanglements that you know to be rather ill-advised is not sensible, and it would be better to wait before you committed yourself exclusively to any one person. It is the essence of your nature to serve the world at large and through doing so it is possible that you will attract money at some stage in your life.

Venus in Libra

Venus is very comfortable in Libra and bestows upon those people who have this planetary position a particular sort of kindness that is easy to recognise. This is a very good position for all sorts of friendships and also for romantic attachments that usually bring much joy into your life. Few individuals with Venus in Libra would avoid marriage and since you are capable of great depths of love, it is likely that you will find a contented personal life. You like to mix with people of integrity and intelligence but don't take kindly to scruffy surroundings or work that means getting your hands too dirty. Careful speculation, good business dealings and money through marriage all seem fairly likely.

Venus in Scorpio

You are quite open and tend to spend money quite freely, even on those occasions when you don't have very much. Although your intentions are always good, there are times when you get yourself in to the odd scrape and this can be particularly true when it comes to romance, which you may come to late or from a rather unexpected direction. Certainly you have the power to be happy and to make others contented on the way, but you find the odd stumbling block on your journey through life and it could seem that you have to work harder than those around you. As a result of this, you gain a much deeper understanding of the true value of personal happiness than many people ever do, and are likely to achieve true contentment in the end.

Venus in Sagittarius

You are lighthearted, cheerful and always able to see the funny side of any situation. These facts enhance your popularity, which is especially high with members of the opposite sex. You should never have to look too far to find romantic interest in your life, though it is just possible that you might be too willing to commit yourself before you are certain that the person in question is right for you. Part of the problem here extends to other areas of life too. The fact is that you like variety in everything and so can tire of situations that fail to offer it. All the same, if you choose wisely and learn to understand your restless side, then great happiness can be yours.

Venus in Capricorn

The most notable trait that comes from Venus in this position is that it makes you trustworthy and able to take on all sorts of responsibilities in life. People are instinctively fond of you and love you all the more because you are always ready to help those who are in any form of need. Social and business popularity can be yours and there is a magnetic quality to your nature that is particularly attractive in a romantic sense. Anyone who wants a partner for a lover, a spouse and a good friend too would almost certainly look in your direction. Constancy is the hallmark of your nature and unfaithfulness would go right against the grain. You might sometimes be a little too trusting.

Venus in Aquarius

This location of Venus offers a fondness for travel and a desire to try out something new at every possible opportunity. You are extremely easy to get along with and tend to have many friends from varied backgrounds, classes and inclinations. You like to live a distinct sort of life and gain a great deal from moving about, both in a career sense and with regard to your home. It is not out of the question that you could form a romantic attachment to someone who comes from far away or be attracted to a person of a distinctly artistic and original nature. What you cannot stand is jealousy, for you have friends of both sexes and would want to keep things that way.

Venus in Pisces

The first thing people tend to notice about you is your wonderful, warm smile. Being very charitable by nature you will do anything to help others, even if you don't know them well. Much of your life may be spent sorting out situations for other people, but it is very important to feel that you are living for yourself too. In the main, you remain cheerful, and tend to be quite attractive to members of the opposite sex. Where romantic attachments are concerned, you could be drawn to people who are significantly older or younger than yourself or to someone with a unique career or point of view. It might be best for you to avoid marrying whilst you are still very young.

GEMINI:
2016 DIARY PAGES

October

2016

1 SATURDAY *Moon Age Day 1 Moon Sign Libra*

Much of what happens in your life right now is responsive to what others have to say. This isn't the most comfortable situation in which to find yourself. Exercise some patience and trust that those you know well will have your best interests at heart. Don't allow the day to become too quiet or you could get morose.

2 SUNDAY *Moon Age Day 2 Moon Sign Libra*

The area of love and romance is now favourably highlighted and should remain so throughout the today. Spending time with the people who are most important to you is essential and should prove to be both stimulating and enjoyable. Try not to be too definite in social plans, leaving some of your options open.

3 MONDAY *Moon Age Day 3 Moon Sign Scorpio*

Although trends today offer few favours, there is extra planetary support about and a general feeling that life is going your way to a greater extent. The one thing you don't lose, even in slight adversity, is your sense of humour. That could come in extremely handy at present.

4 TUESDAY *Moon Age Day 4 Moon Sign Scorpio*

It is close partnerships that make life most fulfilling now, both in a romantic sense and for those of you who are in co-operative professional ventures. Keep a sense of proportion regarding family matters, some of which appear to be giving you a slightly hard time today and tomorrow.

5 WEDNESDAY   *Moon Age Day 5*   *Moon Sign Scorpio*

This is an excellent time to broaden your horizons in a general sense but you could also find yourself making specific journeys to interesting places. Certainly, finding yourself stuck in any sort of rut has no appeal whatsoever. Those Gemini types who can take an extended break now are the luckiest of all.

6 THURSDAY   *Moon Age Day 6*   *Moon Sign Sagittarius*

A mixture of some confusion and not a little incompetence could be the order of the day, so take extra care. The Moon won't do you any favours and you really do need to call on the help and support of others in order to get the very best out of today. All in all, it might be best to stay tucked up in bed.

7 FRIDAY   *Moon Age Day 7*   *Moon Sign Sagittarius*

There are some hold-ups today and there is little you can do to avoid them. Actually, you are taking a sort of devil-may-care attitude, mixed with the type of lethargy that is far from the usual nature of a Gemini. Despite a few negative trends, you should be generally quite happy today.

8 SATURDAY   *Moon Age Day 8*   *Moon Sign Capricorn*

Having moved steadily towards some of your life's goals in the recent past, you now find yourself at some sort of culmination point. That means looking again at issues and deciding where your effort is best concentrated henceforth. A chat with your partner or family members could help.

9 SUNDAY   *Moon Age Day 9*   *Moon Sign Capricorn*

Social and teamwork matters are favourably highlighted now, leading to a feeling that you can get on well with the world at large. Perhaps you are slightly more considerate regarding the feelings of those around you. Gemini is getting quite creative around now, maybe leading to a decorating spree at home.

10 MONDAY
Moon Age Day 10   Moon Sign Capricorn

It is possible that you are thinking of number one at the beginning of this working week. Your sign is sometimes accused of being selfish, though the truth is that you are merely single-minded. It wouldn't do any harm today to remember that there are other people involved in your decisions.

11 TUESDAY
Moon Age Day 11   Moon Sign Aquarius

You are clearly in the market for a good time. Sexy and keen to make a good impression, Gemini puts on its best display at the moment. Don't be surprised if your flirtatious ways lead to encounters you might not have expected. Not everyone you attract is your intended target.

12 WEDNESDAY
Moon Age Day 12   Moon Sign Aquarius

Whilst concentration on the nitty gritty of work could suffer today, instead you are in a positive mood and up for a good time. It won't be easy to do everything you would wish, though you don't feel overly committed to much right now. Gemini loves to have fun and this week is providing that commodity in abundance.

13 THURSDAY
Moon Age Day 13   Moon Sign Pisces

Professional matters should go more smoothly today than yesterday, even if, inside yourself, you would rather be somewhere else. It isn't the things you want to do that matter right now but rather the things you have to do. As long as you keep a smile on your face, the day should prove to be a breeze.

14 FRIDAY
Moon Age Day 14   Moon Sign Pisces

You are still getting to where you want to go, even if the going is just a little tough today. Finding yourself up against it isn't necessarily a bad thing because it adds more drive and greater enthusiasm. Gemini is not a zodiac sign that particularly respects or wants a smooth ride.

15 SATURDAY   *Moon Age Day 15   Moon Sign Aries*

You might find it inspiring to seek out new contacts today, and also gain a great deal from people who figure in your life prominently just now. Personal relationships should also be looking good and you have more than a slight chance of getting ahead of the game in the financial stakes.

16 SUNDAY   *Moon Age Day 16   Moon Sign Aries*

You tend to be more sensitive to outside influences at the moment and this is especially the case if you suspect that there is any sort of criticism coming your way. There are certain things you will have to deal with today, whether you wish to or not, and this fact might put a slight dampener on the day.

17 MONDAY   *Moon Age Day 17   Moon Sign Taurus*

The pace of daily activity seems to have slowed somewhat. The Moon is in your solar twelfth house and the real excitement doesn't pay another visit until after tomorrow. Make the best of what you have today and spend some time planning how you can get ahead from Wednesday on.

18 TUESDAY   *Moon Age Day 18   Moon Sign Taurus*

Your main focus today is likely to be on your domestic life. Not much ruffles your feathers at the moment, though you won't take too kindly to being told what to do. This only really applies if you are working today. Most home-based situations ought to prove distinctly relaxing.

19 WEDNESDAY   *Moon Age Day 19   Moon Sign Gemini*

Things are hotting up again and the presence of the lunar high certainly helps you get ahead. You are now dynamic and raring to have a go at things you shied away from only a day or two ago. If you want an October day on which it proves possible to move mountains, this could be it.

20 THURSDAY *Moon Age Day 20   Moon Sign Gemini*

The friendly assistance that comes from the direction of people you know, as well as strangers, is bound to be especially well received today. This ought to be a bright and breezy sort of day, without too much in the way of perceived responsibility but with plenty of entertainment and fun.

21 FRIDAY *Moon Age Day 21   Moon Sign Cancer*

You are clearly ambitious to get ahead at the moment and there is plenty of incentive about to make this possible. Not only will colleagues and friends rely heavily on your opinions but general good luck attends many of your actions. Leave time later in the day to find new ways to have fun.

22 SATURDAY *Moon Age Day 22   Moon Sign Cancer*

There's a slight tendency for you to play the prima donna today if things don't go your way. Perhaps it would be better to remain quiet and to take stock. Flying off the handle simply won't help and you will only regret it later. The best sort of associations right now are those that exist on a one-to-one level.

23 SUNDAY *Moon Age Day 23   Moon Sign Leo*

Communication with your partner, or someone else with whom you have a particular affinity allows you to get to the heart of matters. In some ways this appears to make the present period a slightly serious one. In reality there is plenty of time for flippancy and fun, though these come once the responsibilities are out of the way.

24 MONDAY *Moon Age Day 24   Moon Sign Leo*

Thanks to the present position of the Sun you will be feeling in a very romantic frame of mind. It isn't hard to find the right words to tell someone how much you care about them and you should be getting a positive response in return. Some friends could seem a little selfish and need special attention.

25 TUESDAY
Moon Age Day 25   Moon Sign Leo

There could well be an element of disorganisation in your life at this stage of the week. Perhaps others are not behaving in quite the way you would wish, or are late meeting you for specific encounters. A flexible attitude on your part will help. After all, what is a few minutes one way or the other? Try to remain patient.

26 WEDNESDAY
Moon Age Day 26   Moon Sign Virgo

Career discussions may not put you in quite the position you would wish. In this sphere of your life right now it's important to remember that when one strategy fails, another is worth trying. There isn't much around that is likely to get you down, though a few frustrations are more or less inevitable.

27 THURSDAY
Moon Age Day 27   Moon Sign Virgo

This ought to be one of the best days of the month regarding leisure and pleasure generally. For the moment you won't be taking yourself or anyone else too seriously. In any case new incentives come along and you ought to find specific friends to be in just the right frame of mind to join you in fun situations.

28 FRIDAY
Moon Age Day 28   Moon Sign Libra

The workplace should turn out to be a place of great harmony today. Work-mates are likely to be both supportive and inspirational, allowing you to push ahead with your own ideas in the knowledge that you have others on board. Arrange an impromptu social outing later in the day and find ways to mix business with pleasure.

29 SATURDAY
Moon Age Day 29   Moon Sign Libra

This is not your luckiest period, even though gains can come along as a result of past efforts. Take life steadily and rely on the good offices of loved ones and friends alike. Confidence to do the right thing might also be somewhat diminished – a sure sign that today is not the time for taking too many chances.

30 SUNDAY
Moon Age Day 0   Moon Sign Libra

A long-standing commitment might need real attention at this time. If so, this could get in the way of what is essentially a socially motivated sort of Sunday. The way forward is to mix and match between what is necessary and the things you really want to do. Balance may not be easy now but it is possible.

31 MONDAY
Moon Age Day 1   Moon Sign Scorpio

Avoid too many hasty or impulsive actions. This is not to suggest that you shy away from making any sort of decision at present, simply that you should think first. People from the past could so easily be finding their way to your door at the moment and happy memories are engendered by many different situations.

November

2016

1 TUESDAY
Moon Age Day 2   Moon Sign Scorpio

Today should be harmonious in almost every sense. Good contacts with useful people could set the day apart and might find you gaining financially from discussions or transactions. Your enjoyment of life knows no bounds, though you tend to express it in a somewhat low-key fashion with the lunar low just ahead.

2 WEDNESDAY
Moon Age Day 3   Moon Sign Sagittarius

A lull patch is now in operation, though is somewhat mitigated by the present position of the Sun, which is quite helpful to you around this time. All the same, this might be a better time for planning than for putting your schemes into action. Be wary of bargains that look too good to be true. They probably are.

3 THURSDAY
Moon Age Day 4   Moon Sign Sagittarius

If you want a day during which you can make a definite impact on the world, this is not it. Instead of trying to do everything yourself, allow others to take at least part of the strain. This does not mean you are likely to lose control, so don't get upset about a fairly compulsory layoff that only lasts a day.

4 FRIDAY
Moon Age Day 5   Moon Sign Sagittarius

Professional objectives do need to be handled especially carefully right now. There are possible defeats in view and you won't take at all kindly to these. Think before you act and if you have any doubt, don't act at all. You will have the chance now to be involved in social gatherings that require little from you except your presence.

5 SATURDAY
Moon Age Day 6   Moon Sign Capricorn

If communication matters have been up in the air recently, you should find them easier today. Gradually, you are regaining your full voice, though this is not a day to be chancing your luck too much. Confidence in situations you know and understand well is high and these are the areas of life on which to concentrate.

6 SUNDAY
Moon Age Day 7   Moon Sign Capricorn

It is easy to tell today how many people hold you in high esteem. You could be surprised at the number, particularly since you learn you are popular with a few people you didn't think liked you at all. Don't be slow when it comes to asking for what you want, especially in a material sense.

7 MONDAY
Moon Age Day 8   Moon Sign Aquarius

Teamwork matters go well and you are at your best when co-operation is necessary today. Although you can be a little offhand with people you don't like, in the main you are charm itself. In the workplace, it is possible that rules and regulations you deem to be unnecessary will get on your nerves.

8 TUESDAY
Moon Age Day 9   Moon Sign Aquarius

An easier-going attitude descends today and might be aided by some very good news coming in for a relative or friend. In your estimation, someone is having a run of good luck you consider to be well overdue. The less selfish qualities of Gemini are on display, which adds even more to your popularity.

9 WEDNESDAY
Moon Age Day 10   Moon Sign Pisces

This should prove to be an industrious period, though there might not be much time for enjoyment. Gemini is on full alert now and making the most of every opportunity that comes along. How important is that though, if you don't manage to have some fun along the way?

10 THURSDAY
Moon Age Day 11   Moon Sign Pisces

You are in a forward-looking frame of mind, still anxious to get ahead and only too willing to take a few chances if necessary. Social relationships are good, though not as positive as romantic attachments. For at least some Geminis, this is the romantic high spot of the whole of November.

11 FRIDAY
Moon Age Day 12   Moon Sign Pisces

Matters close to your heart are boosted today and that sensitivity, so much on display at the moment, is now stronger than ever. Not all your wishes come true right now but you can put in that extra bit of personal effort that will make all the difference. The world might struggle to keep up with you today.

12 SATURDAY
Moon Age Day 13   Moon Sign Aries

You have plenty of personal power now and can have a great bearing on the sort of things that are happening around you. Don't let anyone tell you that you are not influential. The only way to satisfy yourself in anything today is to have a go, and don't be put off by any opposition.

13 SUNDAY
Moon Age Day 14   Moon Sign Aries

There isn't a great deal of logic about today and it appears that at least part of the time you are running on automatic pilot. Although you might find certain people difficult to deal with, you do have great persuasive powers at present and merely have to remind yourself to use them properly.

14 MONDAY
Moon Age Day 15   Moon Sign Taurus

New avenues of communication tend to open up during this, the most potentially interesting of times. Although it might sometimes be further to the winning post that you may have imagined, it's worth keeping on running in almost any situation. The world can be truly yours with only a modicum of effort now.

15 TUESDAY   *Moon Age Day 16   Moon Sign Taurus*

A stable and progressive phase, especially at work, though probably slightly less settled in your home environment. Creative potential is especially good at the moment, though as a Gemini, you may not be a budding Da Vinci. The kind of art you are interested in tends to have a more practical application.

16 WEDNESDAY   *Moon Age Day 17   Moon Sign Gemini*

The Moon races into your zodiac sign, bringing to an end the slightly sticky period you may have experienced during the last couple of days. All is brightness and optimism for Gemini now and if you don't realise this, you are not looking hard enough. Treat awkward situations to a dose of good old-fashioned common sense.

17 THURSDAY   *Moon Age Day 18   Moon Sign Gemini*

Waste no time taking a hands on approach to all vital issues. On this particular Thursday you don't have to stay clear of practical or professional matters. Although there might not be too much time to specifically plan for some fun, simply being at the sharp end of things could be fun enough now.

18 FRIDAY   *Moon Age Day 19   Moon Sign Cancer*

Important issues are likely to come to fruition now and you are getting on well with all manner of people, especially on a professional level. It appears to the world that your mind is clear and that your ideas are sound. This may be the reason why so many individuals are turning to you for advice.

19 SATURDAY   *Moon Age Day 20   Moon Sign Cancer*

Getting specific issues into good working order is possible. Once again you are thinking very clearly and your intuition allows you to look ahead with some certainty. It might be necessary to convince those close to you that you are wise in your judgements. Talking is not difficult today.

20 SUNDAY
Moon Age Day 21   Moon Sign Leo

The social highlights continue and it's clear that this is one Sunday when you will avoid committing yourself exclusively to a sense of duty. You need to be mixing and mingling with as many people as possible. On the way you might meet someone who is going to be extremely useful in the fullness of time.

21 MONDAY
Moon Age Day 22   Moon Sign Leo

The progressive phase continues and finds you willing to make any change necessary in order to make your life run faster and better. You are able to make the best of impressions in a social sense and could even discover that there are a few admirers around at present. Money matters should be stronger now.

22 TUESDAY
Moon Age Day 23   Moon Sign Virgo

Serious compromises will have to be made in friendship. Although you might want everything to go your way at the moment, that isn't how things turn out. Be bold when it comes to making social suggestions because it's quite clear that you have some much better ideas than many of your friends do.

23 WEDNESDAY
Moon Age Day 24   Moon Sign Virgo

A continuing lift in terms of the support you feel you are getting professionally should find you moving forward at a very good pace. There could be some restlessness and a feeling that you would wish to see fresh fields and pastures new. Before moving on in any sense you need to consolidate your present position.

24 THURSDAY
Moon Age Day 25   Moon Sign Libra

Along comes a time for enjoying the company of others, simply for its own sake. You will be less inclined today to hang on to the importance of what your friends are saying. Now you simply want to hear their story because it's interesting. It shouldn't be difficult to attract the right sort of individuals into your life today.

25 FRIDAY
Moon Age Day 26   Moon Sign Libra

Your ability to impress others is particularly well marked today and there's nothing at all wrong with gaining advantage from your natural personality. What you won't take kindly to at present is following what you see as ridiculous rules and regulations, brought about by those who have no real sense.

26 SATURDAY
Moon Age Day 27   Moon Sign Libra

It is possible that you will now find the views of specific people to be quite adamant. If this is inevitably going to lead to disputes or arguments, perhaps it would be best to take one step back. Confrontation will not work to your advantage at present and co-operation is far more likely to give you what you seek.

27 SUNDAY
Moon Age Day 28   Moon Sign Scorpio

What you learn from those around you can be of the most tremendous importance now. Creative potential is good and continues to offer you the chance to break out of old and somewhat redundant ways of thinking. This is particularly true at home, where you could be choosing to make significant changes.

28 MONDAY
Moon Age Day 29   Moon Sign Scorpio

Get as much done on a practical level as you can because there are quieter times ahead. What people recognise in you right now is someone who can cut through a great deal of the red tape that surrounds both you and your friends. Getting to the heart of the matter is clearly what today is about.

29 TUESDAY
Moon Age Day 0   Moon Sign Sagittarius

This is a day when you should avoid taking too many chances with life. It's not only the lunar low, but also the day of the New Moon. That means a quiet phase and one during which you are far more likely to watch and wait. It should be no real hardship to allow colleagues to take most of the strain.

30 WEDNESDAY *Moon Age Day 1* *Moon Sign Sagittarius*

Put a few jobs on the back burner, whilst you sit back and watch life go by. This is not really the Gemini way but it works well for you at present. As soon as tomorrow you will be firmly back in the driving seat but for the moment you can bask in the kindness of relatives and friends, all of whom want to spoil you.

Ⅱ

December 2016

1 THURSDAY   *Moon Age Day 2   Moon Sign Sagittarius*

Group and co-operative ventures probably have very little to offer you today because it is clear you are in a 'going it alone' frame of mind. That's fine, but don't forget that there are people around who could make any problem you come across easier to fathom. It might be foolish to ignore them.

2 FRIDAY   *Moon Age Day 3   Moon Sign Capricorn*

The impact of your personality is strong and enduring, which should ensure that those around you will notice your presence at the moment. If you have Christmas in your sights already, the chances are that you are beginning to realise there is more organising to do that you might have previously realised.

3 SATURDAY   *Moon Age Day 4   Moon Sign Capricorn*

The high-energy period is present and at least some of it is likely to be dedicated to thoughts about Christmas, with arrangements being made all the time now. The social aspect of the holiday is more likely to appeal to you than the tinsel and trappings. Where family members are concerned, you might simply have to pretend.

4 SUNDAY   *Moon Age Day 5   Moon Sign Aquarius*

The power of your personality is especially strong now, so much so that you could overpower others without realising you are doing so. Don't be too quick to judge the actions of others at the moment, especially your friends. In most cases, you should give the people you care for the benefit of the doubt.

5 MONDAY
Moon Age Day 6   Moon Sign Aquarius

Avoid trivia. It's time to concentrate, even though in some senses that is the last thing you want to do right now. Although you are not short of common sense, there are people around who have it as one of their main objectives to fool you in some way. It's up to you to spot them and to take the right action.

6 TUESDAY
Moon Age Day 7   Moon Sign Aquarius

This might not be the best time of the month to expect any form of ego boost. Certain people do not seem quite as keen on you now as they may have been even a short time ago. Part of the fault is yours because you are failing to show the general level of optimism and self-belief that typifies your zodiac sign.

7 WEDNESDAY
Moon Age Day 8   Moon Sign Pisces

There is a certain irrepressible quality about you today that almost everyone is going to notice. There is a distinct possibility that you won't have pushed yourself too hard over the last couple of days. Now, with energy to spare, you are really starting with enthusiasm on the road that leads to a Merry Christmas.

8 THURSDAY
Moon Age Day 9   Moon Sign Pisces

Try to find time to express your inner feelings. In the rush and push of life these sometimes get forgotten. It doesn't take very long to say 'I love you', and these three little words can mean so much. In a material sense, you could find things coming your way that you didn't expect at all.

9 FRIDAY
Moon Age Day 10   Moon Sign Aries

New love could be coming along for some Gemini people, particularly those who have been searching for new beginnings. Confidence is generally high at the moment though you will have your work cut out keeping as many balls in the air as you are juggling right now. Don't forget, Christmas is only a couple of weeks away.

10 SATURDAY   *Moon Age Day 11   Moon Sign Aries*

It is the interesting information offered to you today that keeps you both entertained and happy. Gemini is now very definitely a party animal and you are clearly doing your best to have a good time, even ahead of Christmas. The message of the season isn't lost on you one bit.

11 SUNDAY   *Moon Age Day 12   Moon Sign Taurus*

Your ability to attract the good things in life, and especially money, is noteworthy now. Take whatever direction is necessary in order to get ahead, stopping short only of treading on the toes of others. Socially speaking, the kindest side of your Gemini nature is now clearly on display.

12 MONDAY   *Moon Age Day 13   Moon Sign Taurus*

Your most rewarding moments today are likely to come through personal relationships of one sort or another. There is a distinctly wistful quality to Gemini at present and a deeply romantic approach to life. Keep abreast of events at work but don't try to move any mountains there for now.

13 TUESDAY   *Moon Age Day 14   Moon Sign Gemini*

Though you are certainly not lacking in energy today, the best trends of all seem to be associated with your love life. You seem particularly charming at this time, so getting your own way with the world at large ought to be a piece of cake. In a financial sense, you can definitely afford to back your hunches now.

14 WEDNESDAY   *Moon Age Day 15   Moon Sign Gemini*

As head of your own personality cult, you might even begin to believe your own propaganda today. It's true you are something to see, and looking at you is what appeals to many people at this time. If you have been seeking to make an impression on a specific person, now is the time to turn up your charisma.

15 THURSDAY   *Moon Age Day 16   Moon Sign Cancer*

Emotional relationships now thrive on your natural tendency to show both compassion and assistance. Routines could be rather laborious and may involve you doing the same job more than once but in the main you will be receptive to new ideas and more than willing to talk anything through with loved ones.

16 FRIDAY   *Moon Age Day 17   Moon Sign Cancer*

Social groups and co-operative ventures have much to offer you today. If your mind is on Christmas this would be a good day to lay down some specific plans. When it comes to getting on with others you should have little difficulty. Family members especially are likely to be warm and receptive.

17 SATURDAY   *Moon Age Day 18   Moon Sign Leo*

You now recognise the value of self-reliance and will be going your own way over specific issues. This might mean having to disagree with someone, not a state of affairs that you will relish. Still, there is more than one way to skin a cat and you are clearly quite diplomatic at the moment.

18 SUNDAY   *Moon Age Day 19   Moon Sign Leo*

You can gain a good many favours from specific individuals and tend to show an extremely progressive face to the world at large. With plenty to keep you occupied and a far more optimistic attitude than has been the case for several days, it looks as though you can really enjoy all that is on offer.

19 MONDAY   *Moon Age Day 20   Moon Sign Virgo*

The present emphasis, which is quite clearly focused on leisure and pleasure, should be enjoyable enough. What might be missing today is any tangible feeling that you are making the practical progress that you would wish. This is a double-edged sword because even if most of life is good, you may worry about certain matters.

20 TUESDAY ☿ *Moon Age Day 21 Moon Sign Virgo*

It is important to think things out carefully right now. With just a chance that you might embark on something that isn't too wise, your natural intuition should be your best guide. If this isn't enough you should seek out the advice of someone who is very wise to the ways of the world.

21 WEDNESDAY ☿ *Moon Age Day 22 Moon Sign Virgo*

The level of support that comes in from those for whom you feel a great regard is important at this time. Strangers now play less of a part in your life and even work considerations won't invade your thinking too much. Changes that need to be made at home can be successfully addressed right now.

22 THURSDAY ☿ *Moon Age Day 23 Moon Sign Libra*

Social relationships are probably slightly less favoured now than has been the case for most of the month so far. Try hard to get on with people, and particularly those you will have to rely on heavily later. Confidence isn't lacking, though you need to ensure that you are using it wisely and in the right direction.

23 FRIDAY ☿ *Moon Age Day 24 Moon Sign Libra*

It looks as though you are going to focus very carefully on a specific emotional issue today. That won't prevent you from moving forward progressively or from embarking on a last minute and very necessary shopping spree. Stay in the company of friends when at all possible and cheer up someone who isn't too happy.

24 SATURDAY ☿ *Moon Age Day 25 Moon Sign Scorpio*

As the month has advanced, so you have been slowly building up to what you wanted for yourself and your family. Today shows that acceleration very clearly and might leave you little time to think things through clearly. In many situations, you are running on instinct for Christmas Day. That suits Gemini.

25 SUNDAY ☿ *Moon Age Day 26   Moon Sign Scorpio*

This is a really good day for gathering new information, as well as for interpreting the facts and figures of life in quite a different way. You won't be unduly stressed at present, though one or two family members might be. Try to offer the help you can and provide a listening ear.

26 MONDAY ☿ *Moon Age Day 27   Moon Sign Scorpio*

Since you are clearly open to new ideas today it is important to watch and listen. Something that a friend or relative has planned can be successfully modified by you, though not unless you fully understand it first. Avoid any sort of family dispute and try to spend a little more time with your friends now.

27 TUESDAY ☿ *Moon Age Day 28   Moon Sign Sagittarius*

You should really be willing to slow down the current pace of events. Of course that isn't exactly easy with all that is happening around you. All the same it leaves you time to genuinely savour what the festive season is really all about. Find an hour or two to read a good book or to watch a mushy film.

28 WEDNESDAY ☿ *Moon Age Day 29   Moon Sign Sagittarius*

You should still be feeling distinctly mellow and may discover that the lunar low arriving at this time actually proves to be a blessing in disguise. Although you are not exactly at the front of the queue when it comes to being gregarious, this side of your nature is never very far from the surface.

29 THURSDAY ☿ *Moon Age Day 0   Moon Sign Capricorn*

Though on a personal level it might appear to others that you are quite boisterous, deep inside you are less sure of yourself than seems to be the case. If there is something that you genuinely don't understand, the best course of action is to itemise it carefully and to subject it to intense personal scrutiny.

30 FRIDAY ☿ *Moon Age Day 1* *Moon Sign Capricorn*

This is a day when you could so easily benefit from travel or from allowing at least your mind to wander. There ought to be plenty to keep you occupied on this particular day but you will also be feeling quite restless on occasions. Don't do everything in a totally routine and expected way.

31 SATURDAY ☿ *Moon Age Day 2* *Moon Sign Capricorn*

This could be a day of considerable boons on a material level. You have more than your fair share of good luck, together with a razor sharp intuition and an ability to see what move to make next. You probably won't bother with New Year resolutions. You make life up as you go along and won't change in that respect.

GEMINI:
2017 DIARY PAGES

GEMINI:
YOUR YEAR IN BRIEF

This is likely to be a really good year for Gemini but right from the start you will be quite aware that you'll need to put in some effort if you really want to get ahead. January and February offer you the opportunity to get on top, but not unless you sort things out first. Relationships are likely to feel secure and there could be slightly more money coming your way, especially in February. Be cautious around deceptive people.

March and April could bring you closer to some of your most longed-for successes. Pursue your dreams to their ultimate destination, even if it takes hard work. Throughout both months you should discover that you have more of what it takes to impress the most important people and that you will be quite relaxed in all social settings.

May and June bring the start of the summer, together with a slightly more relaxing and carefree period as far as you are concerned. Now you tend to act on impulse in your practical life and you should be particularly good at turning heads in a romantic sense. It looks as though everyone wants to know you and you shouldn't have any trouble at all progressing in many ways. Set some time aside to devote to charities or help out in your local community.

It seems extremely likely that the hottest months of the year, July and August, will really work for you. A number of different planetary influences come together to offer you better co-ordination, good communication skills and a really strong desire to travel. If you are holidaying at this time be prepared to make some really fascinating discoveries. Trends also suggest that although you might have to work hard to hold on to money, more should be coming your way. Spend wisely and only after due consideration.

The months of September and October bring potential restrictions but these shouldn't hold you up too much if you pace yourself and keep an open mind about everything. Friends will be especially helpful but your partner may not be. At work, get yourself into the right company and don't be against mixing with people you may not have cared for in the past. There are likely to be more surprises in store in late September than at any other part of the year.

November and December will see you once again increasing the momentum of your life. You will know exactly what you want and have a very good idea how to go about getting it. The Christmas period, in particular, should work to your advantage in more ways than one as you enjoy boundless popularity. Look for advancement at work in November and for consolidation of your efforts ahead of the festivities.

January 2017

1 SUNDAY
☿ *Moon Age Day 4   Moon Sign Aquarius*

This New Year's Day holds a slight danger of you dwelling on your own limitations and that is not a good way for Gemini to be. Even on those occasions when you are not absolutely sure of yourself it is important to act as though you are. Romance could be high on your agenda and new possibilities beckon for some.

2 MONDAY
☿ *Moon Age Day 5   Moon Sign Aquarius*

What loved ones have to offer at the moment could seem to be doubly reassuring and since you are not always as certain of yourself as you pretend to be, this is very welcome. The only slight fly in the ointment today could come from having to defer your own ideas in favour of those of a colleague.

3 TUESDAY
☿ *Moon Age Day 6   Moon Sign Pisces*

Certain relationships receive a lift today. Expect to be far more attracted to old and trusted friends than you will be to either colleagues or acquaintances. It might be best not to work too hard today if you have any choice in the matter. A little leisure time works best for you right now.

4 WEDNESDAY
☿ *Moon Age Day 7   Moon Sign Pisces*

There are many possible directions to take just at the moment and since you are spoiled for choice it might be good to seek some outside advice. Once again you turn towards old friends and will also be inclined to talk to wise family members. Trust is a particularly important factor at the moment and is something you understand well.

5 THURSDAY ☿ *Moon Age Day 8   Moon Sign Aries*

You continue to push forward in a very progressive way and will be quite surprised if there are people around who don't automatically go along with your plans. A little persuasion might be in order and since your selling skills are top notch it shouldn't take you long to get just about everyone onside.

6 FRIDAY ☿ *Moon Age Day 9   Moon Sign Aries*

The green light is on, which will please you immensely. No matter what the winter weather is doing you will be happy to be out and about, seeing and doing as much as possible. With all this energy you won't have any difficulty proving to people that you are the right man or woman for the job – just about any job!

7 SATURDAY ☿ *Moon Age Day 10   Moon Sign Taurus*

If there is one thing that is going to get on your nerves right now it will be following rules that you see as both pointless and counter-productive. As a result you could easily fall foul of people who are far more regimented and steady than you are. Accept the fact that there isn't much point in arguing because you will have to toe the line in the end.

8 SUNDAY *Moon Age Day 11   Moon Sign Taurus*

Your thought processes work like lightning and Sunday should offer you a chance to put all this mental energy to good use. What you need most is some fun – and with friends around that shouldn't be too difficult to achieve. Even the presence of the winter weather is unlikely to dampen your spirits at the moment.

9 MONDAY *Moon Age Day 12   Moon Sign Gemini*

The lunar high at the start of this year is most likely to bring an excellent romantic phase into your life. When it comes to impressing someone important you definitely have what it takes to succeed and your attractive nature may even extend in directions you didn't intend. You certainly are flavour of the month and that makes you feel good.

10 TUESDAY   *Moon Age Day 13   Moon Sign Gemini*

Things continue to work out well for you and there isn't much doubt that Lady Luck is most definitely on your side. You have the confidence to do the right thing and the only slight pity is that today may not offer you the chance to move a few mountains at work. Still, there are other, equally fascinating, possibilities.

11 WEDNESDAY   *Moon Age Day 14   Moon Sign Cancer*

You won't mind at all dealing with the dross today and have what it takes to be both rational and steadfast. This is so unusual for Gemini that it will surprise colleagues and might even astonish you. In a social sense you remain as humorous as ever and are happy to be the centre of attention in all public settings.

12 THURSDAY   *Moon Age Day 15   Moon Sign Cancer*

Do what you can to alter things today and don't allow yourself to get stuck in any sort of rut. There is a good chance that colleagues or friends will let you down in some way and it might be necessary for you to work harder in order to compensate for this. Getting to grips with a family issue is your job for this evening.

13 FRIDAY   *Moon Age Day 16   Moon Sign Cancer*

When you are alongside like-minded people you will be happiest of all but you won't derive very much pleasure now from going it alone. Gemini is a very social zodiac sign and you are always happiest when there is something going on. This Friday virtually demands that you take a bigger role in family matters and amongst friends.

14 SATURDAY   *Moon Age Day 17   Moon Sign Leo*

Although you are still very helpful in a general sense there is always the chance today that someone will push you too far or expect too much of you. Your resources run deep but they are not inexhaustible. There will be moments today when you have to address your own needs first and when other people will simply have to wait.

15 SUNDAY
Moon Age Day 18   Moon Sign Leo

Getting exactly what you want from life may not be easy today but have patience because things are going to change markedly by tomorrow. It's time to clear the decks for action and to get thinking. The more spiritual side of your nature is also on display and really begins to show itself by the evening.

16 MONDAY
Moon Age Day 19   Moon Sign Virgo

What matters the most at the start of this particular working week is that you have the ability and the opportunity to do what pleases you. If you have good ideas, which is likely, talk about them to people who have influence and power. You may be slightly short tempered with individuals who you feel are not putting in enough effort.

17 TUESDAY
Moon Age Day 20   Moon Sign Virgo

The sort of people you meet at the moment can be an inspiration to you. Don't be too anxious about situations you cannot control and get on with things you are able to manage. Not everything is likely to be going your way today but when it matters the most you can come up trumps. Give some thought to love now, too.

18 WEDNESDAY
Moon Age Day 21   Moon Sign Libra

Part of your mind is anxious to look ahead and to plan for the future but there is another component of your nature that is more inclined to stick to what you know. You could even be somewhat nostalgic now, which is something you don't indulge in as a rule. You have the power to make someone happy now.

19 THURSDAY
Moon Age Day 22   Moon Sign Libra

Creating a good impression is not at all hard for you at the moment – indeed it has to be said that it is rarely a problem for Gemini. You show yourself to be cultured, easy-going and open to suggestion. Routines are not for you and you will be happiest when you are making all the decisions that affect your life.

20 FRIDAY
Moon Age Day 23   Moon Sign Scorpio

From a romantic point of view you are on top form today and will be devoting a lot of time to showing your favourite person how important they are to you. As is usually the case for Gemini you tend to act on impulse and that can mean that not everything works out as you may have planned. Money matters look good.

21 SATURDAY
Moon Age Day 24   Moon Sign Scorpio

Your winning ways make you popular and could bring you face to face with people who have not played a significant role in your life up to now. Avoid involvement in family rows today, even if you feel as though you should take some sort of stand. Leave others to sort out their own disagreements if you can.

22 SUNDAY
Moon Age Day 25   Moon Sign Scorpio

You want to be as useful as possible to the world at this time but must accept that there are some situations that you simply cannot control. Be on the lookout for individuals who are trying to dupe you in some way and avoid get-rich-quick schemes like the plague. Your confidence is not quite so high now.

23 MONDAY
Moon Age Day 26   Moon Sign Sagittarius

The Moon now enters your opposite sign. This brings the time of the month known as the lunar low. You won't be anywhere near as progressive or certain of yourself as you have been recently and need to recharge your flagging batteries for a day or two. That can be difficult for Gemini to do.

24 TUESDAY
Moon Age Day 27   Moon Sign Sagittarius

Any frustrations that are present today exist not because of the lunar low but rather on account of your response to it. As long as you realise that you sometimes have to watch and wait, there will be little or no problem. Difficulties will arise when you push forward in any case, which is like knocking your head against a brick wall.

25 WEDNESDAY   *Moon Age Day 28   Moon Sign Capricorn*

Some of the assistance that comes your way today will arrive from fairly surprising directions and it looks as though you might be busy with new ideas that can feather your nest in the weeks ahead. The social side of your nature begins to show later in the day and you will be looking for people who share your aspirations and dreams.

26 THURSDAY   *Moon Age Day 29   Moon Sign Capricorn*

Although you are likely to remain busy at work, there are other issues that also demand your attention – maybe to do with your partner or a family member who needs some support. You are in a very charity-minded phase and may also want to lend a hand when it comes to getting things done in your community.

27 FRIDAY   *Moon Age Day 0   Moon Sign Capricorn*

Today you should be full of beans and quite anxious to make as much headway as possible. What others notice the most is how cheerful you are likely to be and just how accurate your assessments are. Rules and regulations will get on your nerves today and what you favour is the chance to make decisions.

28 SATURDAY   *Moon Age Day 1   Moon Sign Aquarius*

Things continue to go your way but there are likely to be moments when you really do need the sound advice of people who are older or more experienced than you are. When specific jobs need doing you will probably have to call in a professional because if you get busy with a screwdriver yourself things could go badly wrong.

29 SUNDAY   *Moon Age Day 2   Moon Sign Aquarius*

If you put all your capabilities together into one big basket you are likely to be more successful in your general dealings than you have been so far this year. It seems as though everything is falling into place at just the right time. Don't be put off by irritating people who do nothing but criticise the achievements of others.

30 MONDAY

Moon Age Day 3   Moon Sign Pisces

You are out there pitching with the best of them today and won't be easily dissuaded from any course of action that seems appropriate to you. Don't be too quick to judge the actions of other people because you might end up having to do far more yourself as a result. It would be best to stick to what you know best – although you won't.

31 TUESDAY

Moon Age Day 4   Moon Sign Pisces

Your level of luck is variable today and it might be best not to push things too much. Everything works out better for you when you are dealing with subjects you understand but too much time spent venturing into the unknown brings potential pitfalls. Affairs of the heart continue to be a very significant factor.

♊ February 2017

1 WEDNESDAY
Moon Age Day 5   Moon Sign Aries

Keep an open mind about all new possibilities, especially in a professional sense. Fortunately Gemini works best on a mixture of common sense and intuition, a combination that can be of great use to you at the moment. Don't get too bogged down with pointless rules and regulations and keep your flair for originality.

2 THURSDAY
Moon Age Day 6   Moon Sign Aries

The romantic possibilities for Gemini look especially good at the moment and you should find it easy to make the best possible impression on others. If you have been on the verge of starting a new relationship but didn't have the courage to ask the right question, now is the time to speak your mind – though in the most romantic way.

3 FRIDAY
Moon Age Day 7   Moon Sign Aries

There should not be anything very complicated going on in your life around now – unless of course you are choosing to get involved in intrigues and mysteries. On the whole you would be better off keeping things as routine as possible, whilst at the same time leaving hours free to please yourself alongside your partner.

4 SATURDAY
Moon Age Day 8   Moon Sign Taurus

Mechanical things might be inclined to let you down for a day or two and you may have to call on the help of specialists in order to keep things moving. Don't put yourself in any potential danger by messing with equipment you don't understand and observe sensible precautions, especially when dealing with complicated machinery.

5 SUNDAY   *Moon Age Day 9   Moon Sign Taurus*

Your responses are far from standard right now and you might find that one of the best ways of getting the attention of important people is to shock them a little. You are sufficiently well balanced not to go over the top but if you do nothing you won't stand out from the crowd. It's important to be noticed for your unique skills.

6 MONDAY   *Moon Age Day 10   Moon Sign Gemini*

Take direct and confident action now. The lunar high brings better luck, a more dynamic approach and an increase in your general charm. Few people will stand in your way today, either because they genuinely like you enough to do what you want or because they are wary of you and dare not argue.

7 TUESDAY   *Moon Age Day 11   Moon Sign Gemini*

You continue to show what you are made of and won't take no for an answer – which is fine for you but rather difficult for some of the people you are dealing with today. Go for gold but at the same time understand that not everyone can keep up with your level of activity or your lightning-quick thought processes. Romance looks good.

8 WEDNESDAY   *Moon Age Day 12   Moon Sign Cancer*

Today may find you in a calculating frame of mind – which means an unsuspecting world had better watch out. There are gains to be made in the financial arena and you won't easily be fooled by anyone. Few people really understand what sort of an adversary you would make but they could be about to find out!

9 THURSDAY   *Moon Age Day 13   Moon Sign Cancer*

A standard approach might not work very well at this stage of the week and you may need to be very original if you want to be noticed. Getting ahead means standing out in a crowd so look for new ways to do so. Once again you have a penchant for anything odd or unusual, and for certain aspects of history.

10 FRIDAY
Moon Age Day 14   Moon Sign Leo

There are some fascinating people about today and throughout the weekend and your thirst for life is difficult to quench at present. Anyone who is different from the norm or who has revolutionary ideas is likely to grab your attention and their presence in your life inspires you to show just how opposed to convention you are also inclined to be.

11 SATURDAY
Moon Age Day 15   Moon Sign Leo

People gather round Gemini now because it appears to them that you have all the answers. Of course this is not the case but you don't have to tell them that. You are more willing than any other zodiac sign to rely on hunch and bluff. Make the most of the weekend, get out in the fresh air and look for simple fun.

12 SUNDAY
Moon Age Day 16   Moon Sign Virgo

Someone you know well but see rarely could make a return appearance – perhaps to your overwhelming joy. However, trends suggest that you should take great care not to create problems in the here and now by seeking to recreate the past. Better to let sleeping dogs lie if possible.

13 MONDAY
Moon Age Day 17   Moon Sign Virgo

Not everyone is going to be on your side at the beginning of this week but that probably won't worry you too much. What matters are the individuals who are following your lead because you won't get too far at the moment without some support. There are new possibilities to pursue in your working life.

14 TUESDAY
Moon Age Day 18   Moon Sign Libra

From a social point of view it appears that you are making the very best of impressions around this part of the week. There could well be an opportunity to mix business with pleasure and it appears that you are being noticed even more than normal. Someone in a position of authority could be calling on your assistance.

15 WEDNESDAY   *Moon Age Day 19   Moon Sign Libra*

All that glitters certainly isn't gold, as you are likely to find out today if you don't pay attention. The best way towards greater financial strength is a steady and continual effort and you won't get where you want to be with short cuts. There are times when Gemini can make a mint by taking a risk – but not at the moment.

16 THURSDAY   *Moon Age Day 20   Moon Sign Libra*

Some satisfying results at work are now likely to be yours for the taking. All that's required is a little extra effort and a cheerful approach to whatever you happen to be doing. Colleagues should be supportive at the moment and may offer you something new in terms of incentive. A good day for signing contracts.

17 FRIDAY   *Moon Age Day 21   Moon Sign Scorpio*

Keep up the pressure, at least for today. You are in for a quieter time ahead so it would be worth getting important tasks out of the way right now. From a social point of view you could be mixing with people who are coming new into your life and you should find that your recent efforts at work are now starting to pay dividends.

18 SATURDAY   *Moon Age Day 22   Moon Sign Scorpio*

Your partner or someone in the family could prove to have some excellent ideas at the moment and you could do worse than to follow their lead. This is the sort of day that offers new opportunities but although you may feel confident that things are going your way, a little care is still necessary for a couple of days. Listen to the advice of a friend.

19 SUNDAY   *Moon Age Day 23   Moon Sign Sagittarius*

Trying too hard is a waste of time whilst the lunar low is around and you would be much better off simply standing back and allowing others to take the strain. Meanwhile take a well-earned rest, while planning your strategy for later in the week. New hobbies or alternative ways to pass the time may present themselves.

20 MONDAY
Moon Age Day 24   Moon Sign Sagittarius

The start of this working week may not inspire you greatly. This is partly because of the lunar low but also on account of family members who seem to be doing everything they can to be awkward. Don't get drawn into rows or even deep discussions – you would be far better off on your own for the moment.

21 TUESDAY
Moon Age Day 25   Moon Sign Sagittarius

Any business deals or new incentives are likely to receive a thumbs-up today. Your vibrant personality sees you on good form and people should take notice of what you have to say. When it comes to negotiations it is clear that you are in the driving seat but you should not push your luck too much yet.

22 WEDNESDAY
Moon Age Day 26   Moon Sign Capricorn

You can make personal advancements by expanding your circle of influence. That means networking and mixing with as many different sorts of people as you can. There could be a feeling about that your optimism is well placed and there could be many opportunities to show off your happy-go-lucky personality to the full.

23 THURSDAY
Moon Age Day 27   Moon Sign Capricorn

Beware of voicing your opinions too loudly today. There is just a slight chance that you will back the wrong horse and that could mean a little embarrassment now or later on. All in all, it would be best to keep your options open and avoid committing yourself more than is absolutely necessary.

24 FRIDAY
Moon Age Day 28   Moon Sign Aquarius

You have the capacity at this time to expand your sense of personal security and will be looking to consolidate gains you made earlier. It is a fact of life this month that you will be looking back almost as much as you look forward. This is not a matter of nostalgia but a desire to avoid repeating the same mistakes.

25 SATURDAY   *Moon Age Day 0   Moon Sign Aquarius*

News that comes your way at the moment could put you in a good position to take informed decisions. It's true that you are keeping your ear to the ground and that you are especially perceptive at the moment. Some might even suggest that you are psychic because your instincts are so well honed!

26 SUNDAY   *Moon Age Day 1   Moon Sign Aquarius*

Mental stimulation that is provided by others is the key to greater happiness and success today. It doesn't matter how much you are tested you are sure to come up trumps every time. A slightly more go-getting phase is underway and if you are the type to be involved in sporting activities, you will feel a great desire to win now.

27 MONDAY   *Moon Age Day 2   Moon Sign Pisces*

Trends suggest a tendency to antagonize others early this week. This is not because of any deliberate intention on your part, but results from the fact that you do tend to have an opinion about everything. If someone else thinks they are an expert it might be kinder for the moment to give way to their expertise.

28 TUESDAY   *Moon Age Day 3   Moon Sign Pisces*

Prepare for a little conflict between some colleagues, or amongst family members at home. It is important that you stay on neutral ground and don't get personally involved in other people's arguments. Set aside some time to listen to a younger person who may have a problem that you can help with.

March

2017

1 WEDNESDAY

Moon Age Day 4   Moon Sign Aries

It may be necessary to keep up some sort of pretence if you want to maintain your reputation now. To many people this would make life too complicated but it's not a problem to Gemini. The only real difficulty comes if you have to tell lies because even you may start to become confused by the stories you have told.

2 THURSDAY

Moon Age Day 5   Moon Sign Aries

Get cracking with things you understand but stay away from complications and mysteries because these will only complicate your life for the moment. Attitude is very important when dealing with colleagues and especially with superiors. The more you strive to build bridges, the better things are likely to turn out for you.

3 FRIDAY

Moon Age Day 6   Moon Sign Taurus

You are still keen to become involved in any situation and to make the most of any opportunity that comes your way. Take time out of your busy schedule to find time to listen to your partner. You don't always give enough attention to your romantic life but if you put aside a little time to do so now, the results could be rewarding.

4 SATURDAY

Moon Age Day 7   Moon Sign Taurus

Although some practical matters may suffer a slight hiccup, it's likely that your love life couldn't be better. With strong supporting planetary influences it looks as though you will be well able to make the most favourable of impressions – either on your existing partner or in the direction of someone you wish was the love of your life.

5 SUNDAY
Moon Age Day 8   Moon Sign Gemini

Now is the right time to take command and to show everyone what Gemini can achieve when it really tries. Good luck is likely to be on your side but in the main you are simply being what you naturally are when at your best. People will love to have you around because you are intelligent, funny and excellent company.

6 MONDAY
Moon Age Day 9   Moon Sign Gemini

News, views and quite definite opinions – that's what people can expect from you at the moment. Your stimulated mind won't be still for a minute and you use every moment in order to further your own ends and those of the people you love. It's amazing just how much one person can get done in a single day!

7 TUESDAY
Moon Age Day 10   Moon Sign Cancer

Dynamic at work and a pussycat at home, that's the way it is likely to be for Gemini at the moment. Look out for anything inspirational and take any opportunity to feed the more refined side of your nature. You are a true intellectual at present and you revel in cultured and beautiful surroundings.

8 WEDNESDAY
Moon Age Day 11   Moon Sign Cancer

Mid-week blues could well come along and threaten to spoil something you have been anticipating. The best way round this is to keep active and to pitch in and help someone else. You will be so busy that you will no longer have time to think about your own lack of sparkle to such an extent that it will soon return.

9 THURSDAY
Moon Age Day 12   Moon Sign Leo

With strong planetary influences pushing from behind, some of the most positive trends of the month come to the fore. What is most obvious is your charm, which you will be putting to good use in a social sense. This might not be the best day of the week for making professional progress but you can at least let your hair down.

10 FRIDAY · *Moon Age Day 13   Moon Sign Leo*

When your intuition tells you to take a specific sort of action it is certain that you should be listening to its advice. You have what it takes to see clear through to the heart of just about any matter and you won't easily be duped or sent off at a tangent. Find out what's going on and arrange your life accordingly.

11 SATURDAY · *Moon Age Day 14   Moon Sign Virgo*

You should be very keen to get new plans underway this weekend but might be restricted by the fact that those around you are not as organised as you seem to be. The time could be right to go it alone or at least to threaten to do so. That should soon make people sit up and take notice. Don't allow younger family members to irritate you.

12 SUNDAY · *Moon Age Day 15   Moon Sign Virgo*

This would be an excellent time for marshalling your energies into one specific project. Don't be too quick on the uptake or you will leave everyone else behind and be willing to listen to what friends have to say. You may not act on their advice but at least you will be better informed and that can really count at the moment.

13 MONDAY · *Moon Age Day 16   Moon Sign Virgo*

You retain a sense of purpose and an obvious determination as a new working week gets under way. There won't be a better time during March to start something new or to travel. It doesn't matter how short or long a potential journey might be, it's the change it brings and the possibilities that it presents that prove to be important.

14 TUESDAY · *Moon Age Day 17   Moon Sign Libra*

In the swing of the new working week, you have everything to play for and it looks as though Gemini will be just as positive as can be. Perhaps not everything will work out quite the way you might have expected, but you are the best person in the world at thinking on your feet. What's more you don't like life to be too predictable.

15 WEDNESDAY   *Moon Age Day 18   Moon Sign Libra*

Get-togethers should prove to be both interesting and rewarding, probably for more than one reason. If there is something on your mind that can only be sorted out by an expert, this could be the best time of the month to approach one. It might cost you money but a problem that could get worse with the passing of time can be solved.

16 THURSDAY   *Moon Age Day 19   Moon Sign Scorpio*

You tend to be very imaginative today and although others might accuse you of ignoring certain obstacles, you can still arrive at your preferred destination. Some people don't understand the way your mind works because they can't exist inside your head. This is just because the world of Gemini is a closed book to less intuitive types.

17 FRIDAY   *Moon Age Day 20   Moon Sign Scorpio*

Keep life as interesting and varied as you possibly can today. Ring the changes whenever you get the chance and don't take no for an answer when you are trying to get someone involved in your activities. New ways of thinking about past events might make you anxious to replay a particular situation again.

18 SATURDAY   *Moon Age Day 21   Moon Sign Scorpio*

This could turn out to be a weekend of contrasts. Things could get boring if you stick around at home, or if you do things the way you do almost every weekend. But simply by ringing the changes you could be in for some excitement. There isn't much doubt about which option you will embrace.

19 SUNDAY   *Moon Age Day 22   Moon Sign Sagittarius*

Keep it casual and personal today and you can't really go too far wrong. This is certainly not the best time of the month to be thinking about major alterations to your working life and nor are you likely to be at your most energetic. Instead, you enjoy hours spent in the company of people who please you just by being around.

20 MONDAY — *Moon Age Day 23   Moon Sign Sagittarius*

With the Moon in your opposite zodiac sign the lunar low is likely to find you less confident, more cautious and altogether quieter than would usually be the case. There is no indication that things will go wrong but since you lack your accustomed belief in yourself you will be automatically quieter and less responsive to opportunities.

21 TUESDAY — *Moon Age Day 24   Moon Sign Capricorn*

Your love life at the moment should be characterised by a great deal of harmony and a good ability to share. Friends are also likely to be quite attentive and will be doing all they can to help you out. It's a sort of mutual appreciation society because for your part you are showing tremendous concern for everyone who is important to you.

22 WEDNESDAY — *Moon Age Day 25   Moon Sign Capricorn*

Even though you will be honest and forthright in all your dealings with the world today you could still be rather impulsive and inclined to cause minor problems for yourself as a result. Your creative potential is especially good and you will instinctively know what looks and feels right, no matter what the occasion.

23 THURSDAY — *Moon Age Day 26   Moon Sign Capricorn*

You have a good flair for dealing with finances at the moment, either your own or those of other people. Family members will be inclined to call upon you for assistance and should receive your help with gratitude. Younger people, in particular, find you a good listener and they will have confidence in you.

24 FRIDAY — *Moon Age Day 27   Moon Sign Aquarius*

Conversations at home are inclined to be harmonious and pleasant. Visits from people you care about but don't often see are likely to take place, and you will also be more inclined to travel under present trends. Practically every event at the moment will help you to feel better about your life as a whole.

25 SATURDAY   *Moon Age Day 28   Moon Sign Aquarius*

You want to overcome opponents today but you won't have exactly what you need to hand in order to do so. If there is any real contest taking place it might be best to stand back and watch because your logic isn't quite what it might be. You could also discover that you are a little clumsy today so watch out for that precious crockery.

26 SUNDAY   *Moon Age Day 29   Moon Sign Pisces*

Today could see a return to the past in some way that is meaningful to you. Family matters and old friendships are likely to be very important to you at the moment and you are in a distinctly nostalgic frame of mind. None of this prevents you from getting ahead in a practical sense though your rate of progress won't be quite as rapid as you would like.

27 MONDAY   *Moon Age Day 0   Moon Sign Pisces*

This is a marvellous time to stand out in the crowd and to show that wonderful personality you possess. People will be very responsive to your overtures and you have everything you need to get ahead in a financial sense. The word balance epitomises your life at present and you also show yourself to be refined.

28 TUESDAY   *Moon Age Day 1   Moon Sign Aries*

When it comes to getting things done right now you will be out there in front and leading the field. To take a subservient position would not be at all inviting because in almost every situation you feel you know best. Family members should be willing to allow you a good deal of leeway but the world at large will be less accommodating.

29 WEDNESDAY   *Moon Age Day 2   Moon Sign Aries*

This would be a good time to develop your own particular style and to show those around you that you are capable of many different forms of action. You know what looks and feels right and won't be inclined to dress according to expectation. Being somewhat different will get you noticed and is a signpost on the way to success.

30 THURSDAY   *Moon Age Day 3   Moon Sign Taurus*

You may tend to underestimate yourself today and this means you may be reluctant to take on jobs that you would normally complete in no time. If you cannot approach a situation with your usual confidence, it might be best to take some time out. If you cannot do so, leave certain things until another day.

31 FRIDAY   *Moon Age Day 4   Moon Sign Taurus*

What an excellent time this would be for living the outdoor life. True it isn't summer yet, but you are quite capable of getting wrapped up and enjoying the good, fresh air. Places of historical interest or cultural significance could prove to be especially stimulating at the moment.

2017

1 SATURDAY
Moon Age Day 5   Moon Sign Gemini

With the lunar high comes a greater desire than ever to get ahead of the pack. If you co-operate at all today it will be from a position of power and influence because you are not going to play second fiddle to anyone. All the same you achieve your ends with so much kindness and charm that people will be glad to see you succeed.

2 SUNDAY
Moon Age Day 6   Moon Sign Gemini

It looks as though you are definitely on a roll now when it comes to getting what you want from life in a material sense. Personal matters are less well defined, probably because you simply don't have the time to stand and talk. Routines would get on your nerves today so keep things fresh and original.

3 MONDAY
Moon Age Day 7   Moon Sign Cancer

It is around this time that old situations begin to break down and some of them will have be to rebuilt in a new way. This is not a situation that worries you much at all because Gemini is always committed to change. With lots of energy around, at least for the first part of this week, you should be ploughing through work.

4 TUESDAY
Moon Age Day 8   Moon Sign Cancer

Your intuition is very strong and will guide you wisely if you allow it to do so. This does mean that you may have to spend just a little time weighing up the pros and cons of certain situations but the wait will be more than worthwhile. Stand by for what looks like being a positive interlude as far as your love life is concerned.

5 WEDNESDAY   *Moon Age Day 9   Moon Sign Leo*

Not everyone will be equally helpful today and you may have to do things yourself that you had hoped that others would complete for you. This is a minor inconvenience and is not worth making a fuss about. By the time you have spoken your mind you could have done the job five times over. Stay calm and cool today.

6 THURSDAY   *Moon Age Day 10   Moon Sign Leo*

Although you may be somewhat more reflective than usual this won't prevent you from making progress in a number of different ways. You seem to have the measure of your adversaries or outright competitors and trends look good for any sporting activity. Good luck is with you at present.

7 FRIDAY   *Moon Age Day 11   Moon Sign Leo*

Curb any impatience at present because it could cause you to do things wrongly or with less panache than is normally the case. There are moments when you should stand back from life and look on in a detached manner. This may only take a few moments but proves to be worthwhile in helping you to avoid making mistakes.

8 SATURDAY   *Moon Age Day 12   Moon Sign Virgo*

The greatest contentment to be found today comes from being in the company of people you both like and respect. Once the responsibilities of the day are dealt with you will probably be looking for ways to have fun and since you are not in the right frame of mind to go it alone you will need to enlist the support of friends.

9 SUNDAY   *Moon Age Day 13   Moon Sign Virgo*

You won't get on too well today with people who insist on being awkward or disruptive. It is fine for you to do almost anything that takes your fancy but you don't always approve of other people throwing a spanner in the works. If Gemini does have a fault it is that you can be rather selfish on occasions – something to work on.

10 MONDAY   ☿   *Moon Age Day 14*   *Moon Sign Libra*

You continue to be optimistic and open-minded in your general attitude to life. This might not win you any prizes but it could get you a new friend or two. The people who really matter to you at present are those who have stuck by you through thick and thin. It might be good today to spend some quality time with your partner.

11 TUESDAY   ☿   *Moon Age Day 15*   *Moon Sign Libra*

It looks as though you will continue to shine when in public situations, even on those rare occasions when you are shaking like a jelly inside. Your ability to give the impression that you are cool, calm and relaxed is a great help at the moment. In social settings a little cheek can go a long way and can get you somewhere very interesting.

12 WEDNESDAY ☿   *Moon Age Day 16*   *Moon Sign Scorpio*

By all means stand up for your rights and for those of people who are less dynamic and self-assured than you are, but exercise a little caution all the same. There is no point in flying off the handle about issues you haven't first looked at carefully. If you are too impetuous you could end up regretting your words and have to apologise.

13 THURSDAY   ☿   *Moon Age Day 17*   *Moon Sign Scorpio*

Avoid tense situations by actively employing the funny side of your nature. You can be the most humorous person around when the mood takes you and this is a sure-fire way to defuse potential problems. Not everyone responds to your charm at the moment but that may be due to a degree of envy.

14 FRIDAY   ☿   *Moon Age Day 18*   *Moon Sign Scorpio*

There are planetary influences around now that could easily lead to a short period of significant inner reflection. Gemini is nearly always on the go and you rarely get the moments of calm and reflection that you need. Today could be an exception in this regard because you seem willing to stand and watch the flowers grow.

15 SATURDAY ☿ *Moon Age Day 19* *Moon Sign Sagittarius*

You want to get on and do things but there seems to be some agency that prevents you from making the progress you are certain is possible. Welcome to the lunar low for April. The only way forward is to stay still for a couple of days. Use this time wisely by planning and organising rather than succumbing to frustration.

16 SUNDAY ☿ *Moon Age Day 20* *Moon Sign Sagittarius*

Things are still likely to be rather quiet and you may decide that the best way to deal with life is to batter your way through situations. Nothing could be further from the truth because you will be up against immovable objects. Let others do the grafting, whilst you call in a few long overdue favours.

17 MONDAY ☿ *Moon Age Day 21* *Moon Sign Capricorn*

It is towards leisure and pleasure that your mind is now inclined to turn and if you are not actually going on holiday it is likely that you will be planning a journey for the not too distant future. You can't stand the thought of being cooped up in the same place all the time and will do almost anything to get some good fresh air.

18 TUESDAY ☿ *Moon Age Day 22* *Moon Sign Capricorn*

Your sense of responsibility towards people at home is stronger than ever and you may drop everything in order to get something sorted out on the domestic front. You will still feel like relaxing whenever the opportunity arises and can do so best when people with whom you naturally feel comfortable surround you.

19 WEDNESDAY ☿ *Moon Age Day 23* *Moon Sign Capricorn*

Inner and spiritual concerns have a good deal to do with the way you choose to live your life just at the moment. Deep questions enter your mind and you will be naturally more inclined towards meditation than would usually be the case. This is not to infer that you have stopped flying about from pillar to post – you have just slowed down.

20 THURSDAY   ☿ *Moon Age Day 24   Moon Sign Aquarius*

Organisation is the key to success today and speed alone simply won't cut it. Things generally are inclined to slow down somewhat, which is probably for the best because it is details that count now. Motivating others today is easy and it is through the efforts of colleagues and friends that you achieve your desired objectives in the main.

21 FRIDAY   ☿ *Moon Age Day 25   Moon Sign Aquarius*

All communications now go extremely well. You can accomplish new skills and should get on unexpectedly well with some tasks. The only slight down side is that your newfound ability might make you wish you had started ages ago. Friends should be seeking you out and especially good to know.

22 SATURDAY   ☿   *Moon Age Day 26   Moon Sign Pisces*

You have plenty of energy but it is still towards your home that you are likely to be looking right now. From an emotional point of view you could be slightly shy and won't find it easy to express yourself in romantic situations. This is strange for Gemini but you can take solace in the fact that actions speak louder than words.

23 SUNDAY   ☿   *Moon Age Day 27   Moon Sign Pisces*

It may seem as though there are lessons to learn from life today. Let's face it, this is a process that goes on all the time, no matter how old you are. What seems different now is that you can put what you learn to good use in a number of different ways. Don't be surprised if you are extremely popular in a social sense today.

24 MONDAY   ☿   *Moon Age Day 28   Moon Sign Pisces*

This would be a great time to improve your efficiency at work because if there is one thing that annoys you it is being obliged to do the same thing time and again. Your mind is always quick but for the moment you are positively ingenious. Take all the components of a task and break them down. Then find ways to speed them up.

25 TUESDAY ☿ *Moon Age Day 0   Moon Sign Aries*

This is a rather romantic time when you can project a sparkling personality and show the world what sort of a person you really are. Not everyone will be in love with you, especially someone who thinks you have sold them short in some way. It's up to you to put this right, probably by showing your generosity.

26 WEDNESDAY ☿ *Moon Age Day 1   Moon Sign Aries*

What a great time this would be for intimate twosomes. You are now slightly more comfortable in your relationships and can express your emotions to a greater extent. This could also be a very good day for clearing some deadwood from your life. New starts are just around the next corner – but then they always are for you.

27 THURSDAY ☿ *Moon Age Day 2   Moon Sign Taurus*

This is a time to exploit any situation that seems to be going the way you might have planned – though in fact you probably didn't. Serendipity seems to be on your side and you are the first person in the world to make use of it. Don't settle for too little when you know that just a little extra effort can get you everything you want.

28 FRIDAY ☿ *Moon Age Day 3   Moon Sign Taurus*

Today you are really appreciating your friends and will do anything you can to keep them happy. This is particularly true with regard to someone who has been going through a difficult time recently. In terms of personal attachments you are now likely to do everything and anything for your partner and the response is magnificent.

29 SATURDAY ☿ *Moon Age Day 4   Moon Sign Gemini*

The weekend coincides with the arrival of the lunar high and there isn't any doubt that you will be up to speed in no time at all. Key decisions can be made and your level of confidence is going off the scale. After a fairly restricted and very relaxing sort of period you are now definitely back in gear.

30 SUNDAY ☿ *Moon Age Day 5* *Moon Sign Gemini*

You seem to be at your best when you are under pressure – though of course you don't notice it as such. The admiring glances that come from the direction of other people should show how much you are respected and you have everything it takes to make the best possible impression. Just stop and take a breath now and again.

May

2017

1 MONDAY ☿ *Moon Age Day 6   Moon Sign Cancer*

You could have a few small problems to deal with today, most likely brought about as a result of the less-than-sensible actions of those around you. Younger family members, in particular, may be taxing your patience and your ingenuity but on the whole there is a humorous side to most of what takes place.

2 TUESDAY ☿ *Moon Age Day 7   Moon Sign Cancer*

Keep up the pressure to change situations to your advantage. Some people may find your desire to do this less than attractive today and one or two may not like you at all. This is not something to dwell on, but instead just accept that no matter how hard you try you can't please all of the people all of the time.

3 WEDNESDAY ☿ *Moon Age Day 8   Moon Sign Leo*

You have rarely been better at dealing with people who are down in the mouth than you are today. Not only do you have what it takes to cheer them up but you are also filled with practical suggestions as to how they can make their own lives better. Just take care you don't end up being accused of interference.

4 THURSDAY *Moon Age Day 9   Moon Sign Leo*

Give yourself a pat on the back for something that has come good after weeks or months of hard work and perhaps take a short break before you pitch in again. Yours is a life that rarely stands still but you can take the odd moment for reflection and to do so is certainly good for you. Family members may seek your advice today.

5 FRIDAY *Moon Age Day 10   Moon Sign Virgo*

Standard responses probably won't work today so try to think of new and ingenious strategies if you really want to get on. Don't be too quick to spend money unless you are certain it is going to work for you. Otherwise you should keep your purse strings firmly tied whilst you wait for a more advantageous time.

6 SATURDAY *Moon Age Day 11   Moon Sign Virgo*

Don't let this be a weekend of absolute normality. If you are really to spark off your mind you need to do different things, maybe in the company of people who don't figure in your life very often. Today is not a time to get tied down by routines and you get on far better when left alone to run your own destiny.

7 SUNDAY *Moon Age Day 12   Moon Sign Libra*

Now you are more inclined to act on impulse, especially when it comes to speaking your mind. That's fine as far as it goes but there are occasions on which you could say too much – or the right thing to the wrong person. You need to be totally in charge of your mouth at the moment and that usually means thinking before you speak.

8 MONDAY *Moon Age Day 13   Moon Sign Libra*

With the start of a new working week comes a day or two of quite intense responsibility. This won't worry you in the slightest because stress doesn't really figure in your life just at the moment. For colleagues and acquaintances things are different and you may have to offer a little timely support at some stage.

9 TUESDAY *Moon Age Day 14   Moon Sign Libra*

Planetary trends now favour social interaction and the ability to get together with fascinating and even stimulating sorts of people. Romance looks good and those Geminis who have been seeking a new love would do well to keep looking now. Help yourself by getting together with like-minded people.

10 WEDNESDAY   *Moon Age Day 15   Moon Sign Scorpio*

The tide should now be turning in favour of greater financial success and gain, though it might not seem that way at first today. Get your thinking cap on because there are definitely ways in which you can help yourself at the moment. In addition you could enlist the support of a friend who is definitely in the know regarding money.

11 THURSDAY   *Moon Age Day 16   Moon Sign Scorpio*

There is no room at the moment to be too satisfied with your own actions or opinions. You can always learn something and adopting an attitude that says you are always correct is never helpful. A little humility goes a long way, particularly to some Geminis. And even if you not humble you could at least pretend to be.

12 FRIDAY   *Moon Age Day 17   Moon Sign Sagittarius*

With the lunar low comes not only potentially the quietest period in May but also the one that paradoxically causes you the least stress or worry. You may not be getting on very quickly but neither will you be especially bothered about it. Accept this as your best chance for relaxation this month.

13 SATURDAY   *Moon Age Day 18   Moon Sign Sagittarius*

Things are now likely to be so slow that you can see through all situations extremely clearly. For everyone else life seems normal but to you it's like seeing things in slow motion. The great advantage here is that you have endless time to plan your future moves and strategies, freed from some of the usual restrictions that surround you.

14 SUNDAY   *Moon Age Day 19   Moon Sign Sagittarius*

You should be fairly content with your lot today and show a happy face to the world at large. Family members could give you good reason to be even prouder of them than you usually are, whilst friends have something important to tell you about future adventures. Don't get unnecessarily jealous about something really silly.

15 MONDAY   *Moon Age Day 20   Moon Sign Capricorn*

There is a strong possibility of extraordinary coincidences and unusual happenings today, which will certainly make you sit up and take notice. It's as if life itself is offering you signposts for the future. What matters is that you read these correctly and adopt the right attitude to benefit from all that could be on offer.

16 TUESDAY   *Moon Age Day 21   Moon Sign Capricorn*

Don't be too quick to criticise the actions or even the thoughts of those who are close to you, either at home or at work. What people need now is support and not criticism. Even though you may be sure that what those within your sphere of influence want to do is wrong, you still have to back them up. Persuasion is fine but never interference.

17 WEDNESDAY   *Moon Age Day 22   Moon Sign Aquarius*

Your opinions at the moment tend to be very down to earth, which is why people are so willing to listen to what you have to say. You won't be elevating yourself in any way and it isn't your nature right now to be arrogant or pushy. Today is about being the best possible type of Gemini and this allows you to get ahead in many different ways.

18 THURSDAY   *Moon Age Day 23   Moon Sign Aquarius*

Your social performance is likely to be impeccable, which is why everyone tends to focus their attention specifically on you. Your dealings with others in a romantic sense are likely to lead to some of the happiest moments. You get the opportunity to show off a little and there is nothing at all difficult about this for Gemini.

19 FRIDAY   *Moon Age Day 24   Moon Sign Pisces*

Affairs of the heart continue to occupy your thoughts and time and for some this could turn out to be one of the most important days for love for quite a while. You are naturally affectionate and caring in your approach to others. This enhances your popularity and should ensure you receive a positive response.

20 SATURDAY　　　*Moon Age Day 25　Moon Sign Pisces*

You have an uncanny ability to get to the heart of just about any matter today and solving problems is as easy as falling off a log. Not everyone will want to have you around, but this may be because they are envious of your personality and your skills. Concentrate your efforts where you know they will be appreciated.

21 SUNDAY　　　*Moon Age Day 26　Moon Sign Pisces*

Your need for communication is strong and cannot be dealt with fully by normal Sunday routines. Rather you need to do something that puts you in touch with people you don't know. What matters the most at the moment is your natural curiosity, which is going off the scale. Your questioning mind will be apparent for most of today.

22 MONDAY　　　*Moon Age Day 27　Moon Sign Aries*

Don't expect everything to work out right first time. You will have to work extra hard in order to get some of the things you want, whilst others will have to wait in the wings until the weekend. Even the best-laid plans can go wrong and if they do you can probably thank those people who regularly throw a spanner in the works.

23 TUESDAY　　　*Moon Age Day 28　Moon Sign Aries*

Now you want to seek out new horizons and to move forward where some of your overall plans are concerned. This would be an especially good day to spend with friends – or certainly in the company of those you like and respect. Your partner might have special needs of you, so save some time for these.

24 WEDNESDAY　　*Moon Age Day 29　Moon Sign Taurus*

The more freedom you experience during the middle of this week the better you are likely to feel about everything. Extended travel would keep a smile on your face and those Gemini people who have opted for a break or a holiday at this time have made the right decision. What you won't want today is to be restricted in any way at all.

25 THURSDAY   *Moon Age Day 0   Moon Sign Taurus*

Right now you show yourself to be a freedom-loving type and you won't take kindly to being restricted in any way. Seeing the world around you and getting out of doors proves to be extremely important and even though you may be expected to work hard today, you also need a certain amount of time in order to recharge your batteries.

26 FRIDAY   *Moon Age Day 1   Moon Sign Gemini*

The Moon returns to your zodiac sign and with it come some of the best incentives you will encounter during this part of the year. There is strong support from planets other than the Moon and your most likely sphere of influence at present is through your work. It seems as though almost everyone wants to know what you think.

27 SATURDAY   *Moon Age Day 2   Moon Sign Gemini*

You continue to pile on the pressure and to move forward progressively. Your nature is charming and the impression you give in almost any situation is certainly going to do you good. With such a bright twinkle in your eye and in possession of limitless charm, you can't fail to also make this one of the most important romantic times.

28 SUNDAY   *Moon Age Day 3   Moon Sign Cancer*

You need to plan the sort of day that keeps you on the move and which doesn't allow any time for you to become bored. You cannot thrive in situations that limit you and Gemini shows itself to be extremely adventurous and even restless around now. Be with friends as much as possible and don't overindulge with food or drink.

29 MONDAY   *Moon Age Day 4   Moon Sign Cancer*

Positive changes within your personal life may occur as you come to terms with the past. You need to be sure right now about what you require and also what you want in order to improve your overall happiness. Conventions are not as important right now as would sometimes be the case for the average Gemini.

30 TUESDAY
Moon Age Day 5   Moon Sign Leo

It looks as though you will be continuing the process of clearing out from your life all those situations and even possessions that are no longer of any use to you. This is spring cleaning on a grand scale and it might unnerve some people close to you. Explaining yourself won't be difficult and you can be sure to carry the day.

31 WEDNESDAY
Moon Age Day 6   Moon Sign Leo

The simple act of taking the initiative, plus a strong faith in the outcome of your present actions will almost certainly ensure success in whatever you pursue today. You have rarely been more confident than you are at the moment and that, too, shows. It may indeed be the factor that convinces others to follow your lead willingly.

June
2017

1 THURSDAY
Moon Age Day 7   Moon Sign Virgo

How wonderful life can now seem to the average Gemini, though not if you spend all your time today worrying and fussing over matters that are not at all important. Keep an eye on the main chance and learn all you can about progress. Maybe you could take a leaf out of the book of a colleague – even one you don't like much.

2 FRIDAY
Moon Age Day 8   Moon Sign Virgo

You might be in a too much of a hurry to complete a specific project today and that could mean getting things wrong. Better by far to watch and listen because the things others are doing and saying could prove to be very informative. This would be a fine time to think about taking a journey – even one arranged at the last minute.

3 SATURDAY
Moon Age Day 9   Moon Sign Virgo

Expect a highlight in your relationship around now and also to be quite keen to get away from routines. An early holiday might appeal but if you can't ring the changes by getting away you could at least decide to make alterations to your home or garden. What matters now is any sort of stimulation.

4 SUNDAY
Moon Age Day 10   Moon Sign Libra

Don't be too quick to judge either people or situations now because some things are not at all as they first appear. The best way to deal with life today is to turn your intuition up to full volume, whilst at the same time employing that Air-sign common sense that so rarely lets you down. The combination works well.

5 MONDAY
Moon Age Day 11   Moon Sign Libra

Stretch credibility a little today when dealing with people who are normally far from surprising. You may have someone quite wrong and if you encourage them a little they could come up trumps in a way you have never expected. Gemini knows a lot about life and people but you are not always the fount of wisdom you think.

6 TUESDAY
Moon Age Day 12   Moon Sign Scorpio

It becomes more and more important to avoid confrontations, especially with colleagues. You may not be quite as sure of yourself as you should be and in any case you can be plain wrong on occasions. The more you push an issue, the greater is the chance that you will end up having to eat humble pie.

7 WEDNESDAY
Moon Age Day 13   Moon Sign Scorpio

The analytical side of your nature continues to be on display and this works for you far beyond the practical world. Working out how other people are likely to behave under any given circumstance can give you a distinct edge and you could shock one or two people when your predictions turn out to be correct.

8 THURSDAY
Moon Age Day 14   Moon Sign Sagittarius

A slower interlude is likely now, though the lunar low this month has the sting taken out of its tail by other beneficial planetary positions. Whilst it is usually sensible to stand and wait when the Moon is in your opposite sign, this time around you can get through or round most obstacles that are strewn in your path.

9 FRIDAY
Moon Age Day 15   Moon Sign Sagittarius

Try not to be too impulsive for the moment and take what life offers without grumbling too much. You are being watched at the moment and the way you deal with little irritations is important. The main stumbling block today may be encouraging a colleague or friend to move, certainly this is much harder than keeping yourself busy.

10 SATURDAY   *Moon Age Day 16   Moon Sign Sagittarius*

You know what you want right now and have many good ideas about how you can get it. The only problem seems to be that others may not agree and this can lead to some sort of confrontation. Avoid this by managing yourself well and turn up your intuition. The important people still love you today.

11 SUNDAY   *Moon Age Day 17   Moon Sign Capricorn*

You have a great regard for the feelings and general sensibilities of those around you and will be finding much more time to spend with family members. At the same time the romantic possibilities are better and you will doubtless be thinking up new and more convincing words of love to write or speak to your life partner.

12 MONDAY   *Moon Age Day 18   Moon Sign Capricorn*

They say that slow and steady wins the race, though this is an adage that might as well be Chinese as far as you are concerned. Maybe you should learn what it means though because constantly rushing today won't get you anywhere. Better by far now to do one job well than to mess up a dozen and have to do them all over again.

13 TUESDAY   *Moon Age Day 19   Moon Sign Aquarius*

The more you alter situations today, the better things are likely to turn out. If there is one thing Gemini hates it is convention. A little upset of the applecart is required in order to bring some more interest into your life. Of course not everyone will approve but if you always waited for approval you'd never get anything done.

14 WEDNESDAY   *Moon Age Day 20   Moon Sign Aquarius*

Any sense of impending doom should be dropped as soon as possible today because you are simply in a more pessimistic frame of mind than usual. By tomorrow everything should be back to normal but for the moment you can expect to feel as though all your efforts are in vain. You have a good flair for the dramatic!

15 THURSDAY   *Moon Age Day 21   Moon Sign Aquarius*

Get together with others, especially for purely social reasons, and enjoy the cut and thrust that comes from simple conversation. You are sometimes so busy you fail to realise that communication is one of the most important components of your nature. It doesn't matter what is being said today because you have an interest in everything.

16 FRIDAY   *Moon Age Day 22   Moon Sign Pisces*

As the weekend approaches you become ever more confident about your ideas and opinions. Whether or not the world at large is as sure of your point of view as you are remains to be seen but you do have good powers of persuasion and it won't usually take you long to convince anyone that you know what you are talking about.

17 SATURDAY   *Moon Age Day 23   Moon Sign Pisces*

Despite the fact that this is unlikely to be the most dynamic or exciting weekend you are likely to experience this year, it can have its advantages. For one thing you will have a little more time on your hands, which you can spend in more or less any way that takes your fancy. Do things today that you want to do – not what you have to.

18 SUNDAY   *Moon Age Day 24   Moon Sign Aries*

There is every opportunity now for you to understand the way loved ones are feeling and to address one or two problems they might have. Have a deeply emotional talk with someone you care about and find out what you can do to make them feel more comfortable and happier. Yours is a very understanding and sweet nature at present.

19 MONDAY   *Moon Age Day 25   Moon Sign Aries*

You have a great capacity for innovative ideas around now and new enterprises can bring a great deal in the way of personal success. There are gains to be made as a result of effort you put in weeks ago and it seems as though one or two ideas you had in the past are now beginning to look far more advantageous than they once did.

20 TUESDAY
Moon Age Day 26   Moon Sign Taurus

In a continuing changeable period, it may not be easy to see the way forward in every aspect of your life. If there is one thing Gemini hates at present it is confusion and so a little frustration could make itself evident today. Just stand back and take stock. Don't rush your decisions and in some cases wait a while.

21 WEDNESDAY
Moon Age Day 27   Moon Sign Taurus

This would be a great time to share your ideas with others, especially at work. It's a fact that you can often be quite ingenious and it is also the case that many of your innovations go unnoticed. That is part of the penalty of being born under an Air sign such as Gemini. However, at the moment you are likely to have an attentive audience.

22 THURSDAY
Moon Age Day 28   Moon Sign Gemini

Gemini is now definitely in gear and very anxious to get on with things. You won't brook any sort of interference and should be just about as pushy and determined as it is possible for you to be. This is a time of potential success and a period during which you can shock and surprise others with your know-how and dexterity.

23 FRIDAY
Moon Age Day 29   Moon Sign Gemini

Keep up the pressure to have things your own way because you are far from selfish at the moment and will make certain that others benefit from your efforts as well. You need change and diversity and would certainly gain a great deal from any journey you chose to embark upon at the moment. Holidays taken at this time really rock.

24 SATURDAY
Moon Age Day 0   Moon Sign Cancer

You should have the chance to meet someone new, probably under fairly surprising or odd circumstances. At the same time you should ensure that you remain as sensitive as possible to the feelings of those around you. Trends suggest that your discretion will be tested. Keep all secrets safe today.

25 SUNDAY
Moon Age Day 1   Moon Sign Cancer

Along comes a wonderful time for improving your mind. Just about anything you learn today will be grist to the mill and you will definitely be on the ball when it comes to putting right the wrongs of the past. You have the chance to feel good about something that has been troubling you for quite some time.

26 MONDAY
Moon Age Day 2   Moon Sign Leo

In terms of money you should now find that cash is available when you need it the most, though there is also a distinct possibility that anything coming in will soon go out again. Imaginative and inventive, you should be able to think up new strategies. Group activities are well accented and friends supportive.

27 TUESDAY
Moon Age Day 3   Moon Sign Leo

What you want most now is to be high in the estimation of specific individuals. In order to achieve this you might have to do things that would normally go against the grain, though nothing will persuade you to lie or cheat. Remember that the most important people have a strong regard for you just the way you naturally are.

28 WEDNESDAY
Moon Age Day 4   Moon Sign Leo

It is now important to organise your life more efficiently than you may have been doing recently. The fact is that you are expected to do well and it is evident that you are the focus of other people's attention. This could make you slightly nervous but there is absolutely no reason why you should be. The only important thing is to relax.

29 THURSDAY
Moon Age Day 5   Moon Sign Virgo

It looks as though nostalgia could be playing a more significant part in your life today than would usually be the case. Because you are looking back so much, aspects of the past will replay themselves. Coincidences make this more likely, together with people and places that crop up out of the blue.

30 FRIDAY
Moon Age Day 6   Moon Sign Virgo

Future prospects look especially good as far as your career is concerned, though maybe slightly less favourable in terms of your personal life. The chances are that your partner, or someone you wish was your partner, will be fractious and unwilling to bend with the wind. For your part all that is required is a little patience.

July

2017

1 SATURDAY
Moon Age Day 7   Moon Sign Libra

This is no time to be rushing your fences. Do it right and you will reap the rewards but if you insist on pushing too hard or in the wrong direction, difficulties are the likely result. Your fertile mind is certainly working overtime at present and you have some of the most wonderful ideas of the year in your head. Defer a few of them.

2 SUNDAY
Moon Age Day 8   Moon Sign Libra

Under pressure to set the seal on some important plans, you might be inclined to change your mind at the last minute in some instances. Nothing is set in stone for you just at the moment but at least you are flexible enough not to worry too much about that. Your creative potential is getting better and better around this time.

3 MONDAY
Moon Age Day 9   Moon Sign Scorpio

If colleagues or friends seem indecisive it will be necessary for you to make most of the decisions. That is hardly a trial for a Gemini but it could be slightly awkward taking everyone into account. All in all it might seem as if life would be much simpler at the moment if you only had yourself to please. It's important to keep smiling.

4 TUESDAY
Moon Age Day 10   Moon Sign Scorpio

This is a very favourable time to involve yourself in new social ventures and a period to wander about more. As the summer really opens up the lure of travel becomes ever more obvious. If there is one thing Gemini hates it is to be stuck in the same place for days or weeks on end, so it's especially important to plan a journey now.

5 WEDNESDAY   *Moon Age Day 11   Moon Sign Scorpio*

With a warm-hearted attitude you will be noticed by almost everyone. It's easy for you to smile at the moment because things are likely to be going your way. At the same time you know instinctively how to please others and will be particularly affectionate towards your partner and close family members.

6 THURSDAY   *Moon Age Day 12   Moon Sign Sagittarius*

As the Moon moves into your opposite sign, so you have slightly less energy than before and will be fairly happy to sit still from time to time. As a rule this doesn't please you at all because it is the essence of your nature to be always on the go. But for now what you probably want most is a comfortable chair and a really good book.

7 FRIDAY   *Moon Age Day 13   Moon Sign Sagittarius*

You might not be quite as precise as necessary at the moment because the lunar low this time around is almost certain to make you a little vague and slipshod. All the same, its power to have any great bearing on your life is limited and you can afford to coast through the Moon's residence in your opposite zodiac sign because others will take the strain.

8 SATURDAY   *Moon Age Day 14   Moon Sign Capricorn*

Personal encounters are especially important and they offer the very best of what life has in store for you. Don't be too quick to follow the lead of someone who you know to be either confused or downright wrong. It's up to you to steer people in the right direction – with a mixture of simple psychology and gentle pressure.

9 SUNDAY   *Moon Age Day 15   Moon Sign Capricorn*

Romance is on the rise and it tends to come your way when you least expect it. Gemini is very attractive to others but can also be quite naive on occasions. As a result you could find that you have some unexpected admirers. Keep a sense of proportion when it comes to spending money, at least until the middle of the week.

10 MONDAY
Moon Age Day 16   Moon Sign Capricorn

Today you are likely to deal more in possibilities than in certainties, though your hunches are generally very good and you can at least afford to explore a few options. Don't get too tied down with any one task, especially if it is something you see as being tedious. Leave it until another day while you have fun.

11 TUESDAY
Moon Age Day 17   Moon Sign Aquarius

Focus on material priorities today, mostly because you have been ignoring them of late. That doesn't mean you should sit and paw over the family accounts all day and you can certainly afford to split your time so that at least some hours are spent doing enjoyable things. Sporting activities could bring greater success than you might have expected.

12 WEDNESDAY
Moon Age Day 18   Moon Sign Aquarius

All matters of communication go well for you and there is a distinct possibility that you will want to get on side with people you haven't instinctively liked much in the past. Yours is probably the most flexible of all the zodiac signs and it is possible for you to be a very different person on any two consecutive days.

13 THURSDAY
Moon Age Day 19   Moon Sign Pisces

Obligations that you feel today may prevent you from doing exactly as you would wish but you may end up surprised how enjoyable routine tasks turn out to be. Money matters are likely to be getting better, perhaps as a result of your actions in the past. Follow up on new and revolutionary ideas that come into your head around now.

14 FRIDAY
Moon Age Day 20   Moon Sign Pisces

It is likely that you will be applying yourself very positively at the moment, whilst it seems as if just about everyone else is talking about work rather than getting on with it. Never mind, if you want anything doing properly you will most likely have to do it yourself in any case. Routines can be something of a bind at present.

15 SATURDAY   *Moon Age Day 21   Moon Sign Aries*

Standard responses in personal attachments most likely won't work and you will have to put in some extra effort to please your partner or sweetheart. This won't be too much of a problem except for the fact that, as always, you are busy doing other things. Make a conscious decision to spoil your lover in some way and then don't forget.

16 SUNDAY   *Moon Age Day 22   Moon Sign Aries*

Personal finances are likely to be very secure today and you can find ways to make more money in the weeks and months ahead. All it takes is a little initiative now, together with a good deal of co-operation and some startling plans for the future. Don't let anyone put you off a course of action you know to be correct.

17 MONDAY   *Moon Age Day 23   Moon Sign Aries*

You could well spend so much time today thinking about changes you want to make that in the end very little actually gets done. Make sure that necessary tasks are dealt with early in the day and at least that will give you more time later to mull things over. Rules of one sort or another could easily get on your nerves at present.

18 TUESDAY   *Moon Age Day 24   Moon Sign Taurus*

Around this time home and family becomes extremely important to Gemini. Take a happy trip down memory lane with family members and enjoy the time spent with them. Someone younger may be turning to you for specific advice, which you will be only too pleased to offer at this time.

19 WEDNESDAY   *Moon Age Day 25   Moon Sign Taurus*

In-depth discussions could be the order of the day and you will be looking at certain matters far more seriously than you were doing even a couple of days ago. You want to have everything just right and will go to tremendous trouble in order to be satisfied with your efforts. Unfortunately not everyone is quite so conscientious today.

20 THURSDAY　　*Moon Age Day 26　Moon Sign Gemini*

Today starts on a good note as the lunar high brings newer and better opportunities into your life. You are likely to have a good deal of simple luck on your side but much of your success today is down to being in the right place at the right time. People generally should be easier to deal with around now.

21 FRIDAY　　*Moon Age Day 27　Moon Sign Gemini*

There are a number of gains to be made today and most of them come as a result of your very dynamic approach to life in a general sense. You show yourself to be ingenious whilst at the same time maintaining a cheerful and attractive attitude. This is the time of the month to catapult yourself into new and fascinating relationships.

22 SATURDAY　　*Moon Age Day 28　Moon Sign Cancer*

Love and romantic issues are now likely to be very rewarding and there is more room in your life for self-expression. Creative pursuits are also likely to go well for you and there is a feeling around that you want to make significant changes to your home environment. Before you spend a fortune make sure of what you really want.

23 SUNDAY　　*Moon Age Day 0　Moon Sign Cancer*

Though you may feel quite happy with your lot in a general sense, your over-riding desire is to feel useful and able to accomplish some of your most important objectives. These may not be large or seemingly earth-shattering but if they are significant to you, that is enough. Listen to what friends are saying this evening.

24 MONDAY　　*Moon Age Day 1　Moon Sign Leo*

You should be talkative and quick-witted today, which makes you fun to have around and popular with your friends. Colleagues may not be quite as helpful as you might wish but you can bring them round with a little effort. By the evening you could be in the mood for some romance and will be doing all you can to impress in a social sense.

25 TUESDAY
Moon Age Day 2   Moon Sign Leo

Others may disagree with what you say or more to the point what you are thinking. Whether you decide to be quite as truthful as would usually be the case depends on the situation and the adage 'discretion is the better part of valour' may be uppermost in your mind. You may not take kindly to being told what to do by a subordinate.

26 WEDNESDAY
Moon Age Day 3   Moon Sign Virgo

Prioritise your cultural interests and feed the deeper qualities of your mind. If you are able to get out of the house today you will probably find happiness in anything historical or refined. Dirty jobs or conflict with others are most displeasing to you now. You are very contemplative at the moment.

27 THURSDAY
Moon Age Day 4   Moon Sign Virgo

You should find yourself getting to the very heart of discussions with a very definite point of view. What matters however is that you are not forcing your opinions down the throats of anyone else, and that will increase your popularity no end. The time has also come to steal a march over a competitor.

28 FRIDAY
Moon Age Day 5   Moon Sign Libra

Although you continue to be in the know where all new ideas and incentives are concerned, at the same time you remain fairly laid back in your attitude. Although you have strong opinions you are unlikely to express them much for today, though things are likely to alter markedly tomorrow. For now simply enjoy the ride.

29 SATURDAY
Moon Age Day 6   Moon Sign Libra

This is likely to be one of the very best times of the year to make important decisions that affect your living situation or life circumstances generally. Others should be more than willing to support any decision you make and your sense of occasion is especially good right now. This is a day to shine and to force others to like you.

30 SUNDAY
Moon Age Day 7   Moon Sign Libra

This would be a very favourable time to eliminate non-essentials and to start new regimes that you know are going to see you getting on better in a material sense. There are plenty of suggestions on the table, many of them coming from colleagues and family members but in the end you choose your own way forward.

31 MONDAY
Moon Age Day 8   Moon Sign Scorpio

Typically you are likely to be quite candid in your manner today and you certainly won't be suffering fools gladly. You will prefer to mix with individuals who have a very positive attitude to life and who make up their minds quickly – as of course you do. However, even slower and more deliberate people have things to say.

2017

1 TUESDAY
Moon Age Day 9   Moon Sign Scorpio

Social relationships should prove to be fairly exciting at the moment and you could even be moving with an entirely different set of people to the ones you depend upon for most of the time. In every sense you are moving quickly towards your chosen objectives and you are likely to be quite specific in your aims and ambitions.

2 WEDNESDAY
Moon Age Day 10   Moon Sign Sagittarius

It's true that energy will be in short supply today and that you won't feel like pushing yourself too hard. With the lunar low around you may settle more easily for a seat in the sun or for cruising around in the car to some place you love. Don't have too many practical expectations at the moment and you can't go far wrong.

3 THURSDAY
Moon Age Day 11   Moon Sign Sagittarius

Although this won't be the most positive period that you are ever likely to experience, things can still work out well for you in a general sense. Just don't expect too much and avoid taking on more than you know you can handle. This is a time to recharge your batteries and not a period for burning yourself out.

4 FRIDAY
Moon Age Day 12   Moon Sign Sagittarius

Your competitive attitude when in social settings could provoke some tension between yourself and others. You may also need to give those around you the benefit of the doubt just at the moment, even if you suspect in your heart of hearts that they are working against your own best interests.

121

5 SATURDAY   *Moon Age Day 13   Moon Sign Capricorn*

Your general daily routines could be affected by small mishaps, leading you to a situation that means repeating yourself. You may also overrate the possibility of a lucky break coming along at just the right time because in the main you will only get out what you put in around now. There is luck – but you manufacture it yourself.

6 SUNDAY   *Moon Age Day 14   Moon Sign Capricorn*

This is a fairly progressive period but one that is more likely to be dedicated to planning rather than doing. Getting yourself organised should prove to be easy, even if others are looking on rather than helping you out. Stay your hand for the moment because the real action comes further down the line. Family ties prove important now.

7 MONDAY   *Moon Age Day 15   Moon Sign Aquarius*

Change and movement is important for Gemini at the best of times but is fairly crucial at the moment. There are gains to be made from following unusual ideas and from pursuing something that others see as a lost cause. The fact is that you simply won't be beaten right now and that gets you noticed all the more.

8 TUESDAY   *Moon Age Day 16   Moon Sign Aquarius*

You are unlikely to be entirely satisfied with anything today – that is unless you get the chance to sort it out for yourself. You don't trust others at the moment and will be very picky when you are following in the footsteps of another. However, even Gemini must learn to trust and to take some things at face value. Remain adventurous today.

9 WEDNESDAY   *Moon Age Day 17   Moon Sign Pisces*

Your love life and matters of romance should be highly rewarding just now and today may well prove to be one of the happiest and most contented days of the month so far. While the weather is good, spend time relaxing – though even this can be a very dynamic and strenuous experience for Gemini at present. Spoil your lover today.

10 THURSDAY *Moon Age Day 18 · Moon Sign Pisces*

Now you are at your very best when dealing with practical matters and on those occasions when things are left to you to be sorted out once and for all. People trust you and your commitment to the task at hand means you won't let anyone down. Beware that this does not also lead to a little too much intensity.

11 FRIDAY *Moon Age Day 19 · Moon Sign Pisces*

Today should be fairly satisfying but can have its problems if you refuse to show a more easy-going attitude to life generally. Little things that others do could so easily annoy you and may cause you to be somewhat grumpy on occasions. Be positive to people you know in your heart are only trying to help.

12 SATURDAY *Moon Age Day 20 · Moon Sign Aries*

You could now feel mistrustful and vulnerable regarding a personal matter. Although you want to trust other people their actions are such that this becomes quite difficult. It is possible that you have got hold of the wrong end of the stick and a complete reappraisal of the situation may be in order at some stage today.

13 SUNDAY ☿ *Moon Age Day 21 · Moon Sign Aries*

It looks as though you will continue to make steady progress towards your career goals – but when was 'steady progress' ever enough for a Gemini? All the same, you could find that things begin to go wrong if you really put on the pressure and would be well advised to pace yourself in almost anything you do. Look for new social interests.

14 MONDAY ☿ *Moon Age Day 22 · Moon Sign Taurus*

If it seems that your love life and romantic matters generally are in the doldrums at present you will have to put in some extra effort. Even then you might not be at your happiest with those around you. Friends may bring you greater satisfaction than your lover or family members but this is a very temporary state of affairs.

15 TUESDAY ☿ *Moon Age Day 23 Moon Sign Taurus*

This should be a first class time from a professional point of view, if only because you are showing everyone just how capable you can be. Recent efforts should pay off well and people should take notice of what you have to say. The same may not be entirely true at home, where certain relatives might choose to ignore you.

16 WEDNESDAY ☿ *Moon Age Day 24 Moon Sign Gemini*

Along comes an excellent time to put your luck to the test. The August lunar high is likely to be very potent and whilst it might not bring you your heart's desire, it can go a long way in that direction. All that's required in some cases is the finishing touch and you tend to put full stops to situations quite easily today.

17 THURSDAY ☿ *Moon Age Day 25 Moon Sign Gemini*

Life should continue to be going your way, which at the moment tends to be the way you choose. You can certainly benefit from putting new ideas to the test and will be happy to take other people along with you on whatever adventure takes your present fancy. This would be the best time of the month for a holiday.

18 FRIDAY ☿ *Moon Age Day 26 Moon Sign Cancer*

There seems to be no reason why life should let you down in any major way, though today might not turn out to be quite as exciting or eventful as you may have wished. It could be slightly harder than usual to get anything done and you may also have to sort out the odd mess made by a colleague or friend. Romance does look good now.

19 SATURDAY ☿ *Moon Age Day 27 Moon Sign Cancer*

This would be a good day for discussions, especially those that take place in or around your home. You will want to get the opinions of those closest to you about ideas you have for alterations to your house or garden – though it is important to genuinely take their opinions on board. Don't simply nod and then do what you want anyway.

20 SUNDAY ☿ *Moon Age Day 28 Moon Sign Leo*

There are likely to be deep and intense reactions with others at this time. You have may have an important message to convey and could be keen to show people how you really feel about a specific issue. There are times when you could be slightly over dramatic but as usual you communicate well and leave everyone feeling good.

21 MONDAY ☿ *Moon Age Day 29 Moon Sign Leo*

Today is ideal for getting out and about and you will be anxious to get as much done early in the day as you possibly can. This is because you have a rather crowded schedule and will need every moment to get through a host of jobs. You can now enjoy a more expansive lifestyle and won't want your horizons restricted.

22 TUESDAY ☿ *Moon Age Day 0 Moon Sign Virgo*

When it comes to work it looks as though someone might be trying to take the wind out of your sails. The chances are that they think they are helping but that's not the way it looks from your perspective. There are advantages to being there first, no matter what you take on, so don't hang about and always be on time today.

23 WEDNESDAY ☿ *Moon Age Day 1 Moon Sign Virgo*

Now you are impatient to get down to basics and overcome any recent delays. You won't have time for anyone who stands in your way or who tries to complicate things for you. In personal attachments you are creating the best possible impression and will be doing all you can to please people on the social scene.

24 THURSDAY ☿ *Moon Age Day 2 Moon Sign Virgo*

To achieve professional success now it is necessary to be both objective and optimistic. Don't be limited by what others think and, where possible, plough your own furrow at the moment. Someone in authority could prove to be especially helpful and you may feel more inclined to co-operate than you have for a few days.

25 FRIDAY ☿ *Moon Age Day 3   Moon Sign Libra*

It would seem that the best thing you can do today is remain active, but not to the extent that you have exhausted yourself by the middle of the day. Most independent actions and new initiatives will bring significant success and first class results can be achieved by looking at old situations in a new and slightly revolutionary way.

26 SATURDAY ☿ *Moon Age Day 4   Moon Sign Libra*

You can really express your ideas today and will be chatting on about one thing or another from the very moment you get out of bed. You are likely to be friendly in social situations but will be just as approachable at work. Try to make a friend out of someone who has been difficult to deal with at times in the recent past.

27 SUNDAY ☿ *Moon Age Day 5   Moon Sign Scorpio*

Now you sense that something quite significant is just around the corner. Although you may still be thinking quite deeply about life you will have more savvy and a greater desire for active participation. Old and worn-out concepts may be dumped before the end of today in favour of a more streamlined attitude.

28 MONDAY ☿ *Moon Age Day 6   Moon Sign Scorpio*

New personalities enter your life at every stage and there is not one sphere of your existence that isn't potentially suffused with greater excitement now. Conventions don't really appeal to you at the moment and everything about you seems to be geared towards the future. At the same time you will still need more rest than usual.

29 TUESDAY ☿ *Moon Age Day 7   Moon Sign Sagittarius*

You can now further your aims and ambitions through new information that seems to be coming your way all the time. People in positions of influence will once again prove how useful they can be to you, though at least a part of your day should be spent doing things that are not so much important as just simply interesting.

30 WEDNESDAY ☿ *Moon Age Day 8   Moon Sign Sagittarius*

You can now do much to make improvements to your life in a general sense, though there isn't much doubt that most of your efforts today will be geared towards home and family. Not that you are retreating from the world at all. On the contrary you are getting involved in more activities than even Gemini is inclined to do as a rule.

31 THURSDAY ☿ *Moon Age Day 9   Moon Sign Sagittarius*

You can benefit from a fairly high professional profile and from being in the right place at any given point in time. You are a natural leader in your field and will be called upon by others on a regular basis. There is a great deal of advantage in sharing and discussing matters today – even with people who are very different from yourself.

1 FRIDAY
☿ *Moon Age Day 10   Moon Sign Capricorn*

There could be certain pressures brought to bear on you today and most of these are likely to come from home. Professional matters appear to be more successful than personal ambitions and it is therefore towards your work that you are now most likely to turn. It could seem as if almost everyone is going on about something.

2 SATURDAY
☿ *Moon Age Day 11   Moon Sign Capricorn*

This is quite simply going to be one of the best days of the month for being with others and for getting on well with life generally. You enjoy good company and will be quite happy to surround yourself with luxury if that proves to be possible. Responsibilities don't bother you much under present planetary trends.

3 SUNDAY
☿ *Moon Age Day 12   Moon Sign Aquarius*

You might still be slightly lacking in conviction and respond best when everyone tells you how right you are. Although to the world at large Gemini might seem to be the most self-assured and confident person in the world, this is not always the case. But at least you give a good impression and sometimes that is enough.

4 MONDAY
☿ *Moon Age Day 13   Moon Sign Aquarius*

If there is a fly in the ointment today it is likely to be that family relationships are not quite as strong as you might wish them to be. This state of affairs is unlikely to be your fault, though you can do something towards sorting it out. Don't get too tied down with details today because a broad overview will work best for you.

5 TUESDAY   ☿ *Moon Age Day 14   Moon Sign Aquarius*

Trends suggest that you now enjoy the trust and support of those around you – in particular people you work with. It's good to know that you have their confidence but you may also be enjoying or enduring extra work as a result. This might be because you are such a willing horse and the way out of it is to delegate more than you are doing.

6 WEDNESDAY   ☿   *Moon Age Day 15   Moon Sign Pisces*

This may not be the best time for logical planning and it looks as though you will be happiest when you can make up your mind on the spur of the moment. People tend to gather round you at present and it is likely that you are on the receiving end of compliments, which is always a good psychological spur to a Gemini.

7 THURSDAY   ☿   *Moon Age Day 16   Moon Sign Pisces*

It's time to get down to business and to deal with a few issues that might have been put on the back burner for a week or two. Your organisational skills are now particularly good and it won't be difficult to get colleagues, friends or family members to accept their own responsibilities. The sign of the Twins is definitely in charge.

8 FRIDAY   ☿   *Moon Age Day 17   Moon Sign Aries*

Stand by for a sudden and quite mysterious lack of confidence regarding a specific matter. This won't last long and in reality might turn out to be a storm in a teacup but it could have a bearing on your decision-making during the first part of the day. You respond very positively to the cheerful attitude of family members at this time.

9 SATURDAY   ☿   *Moon Age Day 18   Moon Sign Aries*

Almost certainly you will now be getting the very best from romantic attachments and from all forms of relationship that have no professional connection. If you are working today you might feel slightly less secure and may be quite willing to allow colleagues to make the running. The fact is that you are somewhat less interested in your ambitions now.

10 SUNDAY ☿ *Moon Age Day 19   Moon Sign Taurus*

A few unexpected delays could hold you back at first today but these tend to be dealt with one at a time and without undue panic. You respond well to any sort of demand that is made of you at the present time but will remain quite aware that today offers social and personal possibilities. Your mind is well balanced and fairly serene.

11 MONDAY ☿ *Moon Age Day 20   Moon Sign Taurus*

Your attitude at the moment is noteworthy and the only thing that is missing is that element of good luck that normally follows you around. As a result you will have to work harder to get what you want and may also find obstacles being thrown in your path. Fortunately social and romantic trends are better and tomorrow begins to be generally good.

12 TUESDAY ☿ *Moon Age Day 21   Moon Sign Gemini*

Make an early start today and get on with doing something that really pleases you, as well as being of financial or practical benefit. There is really no limit to your capabilities at this time and you could discover that you are very much better at something than you expected to be. Gemini is also very competitive today.

13 WEDNESDAY *Moon Age Day 22   Moon Sign Gemini*

You could receive a reminder today that things are far better than you might have expected. The fact is that the lunar high offers you all the support you could possibly need and you are going to be in the most positive frame of mind that you will experience in the whole month of September. Use these advantages.

14 THURSDAY *Moon Age Day 23   Moon Sign Cancer*

You can now get a great deal done and as well as achieving your own objectives you may help others to do the same. Spend some time with your partner or lover and make it plain just how important they are to you. When it comes to dreaming up inspirational social activities you are top of the tree during this particular Thursday.

15 FRIDAY   *Moon Age Day 24   Moon Sign Cancer*

It will seem as though you have to work extra hard today in order to get to your objectives but the effort can be more than worthwhile. You are having some very good ideas and it only takes a little effort to make some of these into concrete realities. Enlist the support of colleagues at work and friends closer to home.

16 SATURDAY   *Moon Age Day 25   Moon Sign Cancer*

Renew your energy today through almost any sort of creative pursuit. The main gain probably comes through love and romance and there isn't any doubt about your ability to turn heads. New projects of one sort or another should appeal to you at this stage of the weekend and your approach is entirely Gemini.

17 SUNDAY   *Moon Age Day 26   Moon Sign Leo*

Your strength of character is likely to be challenged by the forces of repression today. Broadly speaking this means you are going to be restricted in your own ideas and may have to follow the dictates of others. This won't please you in the slightest and it is clear that some sort of confrontation becomes more and more likely.

18 MONDAY   *Moon Age Day 27   Moon Sign Leo*

You may now decide that the time is right to assess your life progress in a general sense. This isn't too unusual for Gemini and is a process that is very necessary to your intellectual makeup. All the same you could discover that you are carrying a certain amount of unnecessary baggage and may decide something has to go!

19 TUESDAY   *Moon Age Day 28   Moon Sign Virgo*

In a professional sense it appears that you are holding a very good set of cards at present. And that's the way business is likely to look – as if it were a game of poker. You won't want to make others aware of what you know but at the same time you would be happier having them on your side. Play it shrewd and cunning today.

20 WEDNESDAY
Moon Age Day 0   Moon Sign Virgo

Your greatest satisfaction at the moment is likely to come as a result of your interaction with others. You need to be the centre of attention and will be doing almost anything necessary to get yourself noticed. Confidence remains generally high but be aware of opponents about and stay on your guard.

21 THURSDAY
Moon Age Day 1   Moon Sign Libra

When it comes to making practical decisions today you may need to exercise more care and to show others how well you can concentrate on the matter at hand. Don't get tied up in red tape and wherever possible look for new ways to do things. It is your refreshingly candid attitude that attracts others around this time.

22 FRIDAY
Moon Age Day 2   Moon Sign Libra

People find you easy to get along with and it is true that you are very easy going and good to have around. The great advantage of the Gemini nature is that you can adapt to suit changing circumstances and different people. All the same if there were someone who is trying to rile you it would be best to ignore them altogether.

23 SATURDAY
Moon Age Day 3   Moon Sign Scorpio

It's good to be with people you care for but you may feel slightly torn because you still want to concentrate on practical matters. All the same there are people who need you and you recognise this early in the day. It may be necessary to carefully compartmentalise your day so that nothing gets left out. Romance blossoms later.

24 SUNDAY
Moon Age Day 4   Moon Sign Scorpio

Activities involving teamwork go well at this time and Sunday offers a variety of different possibilities. You will probably be quite willing to drop the traces of responsibility for a day or two and as a result you become more approachable in a social sense. Concentrate on pleasing those very people upon whom your happiness depends.

25 MONDAY
Moon Age Day 5   Moon Sign Scorpio

It is a fact at the start of this week that you will be easily distracted and much less inclined than you have been to concentrate on specific tasks. It seems as if there is so much out there to take your interest that the hard realities of life are suddenly of little importance. Treat today as a little holiday and get back in gear tomorrow.

26 TUESDAY
Moon Age Day 6   Moon Sign Sagittarius

A planetary lull comes into operation and you won't help your cause by trying harder than is strictly necessary to do anything. On the contrary you would be far better off watching and waiting, whilst you allow other people to do most of the work. Trust in their abilities to get things right and to work on your behalf.

27 WEDNESDAY
Moon Age Day 7   Moon Sign Sagittarius

You might tend to be rather too impulsive for your own good just now and should definitely avoid signing documents or taking on financial commitments you haven't explored fully. Better by far to delay most important decisions when you can or to let someone you trust decide on something that puzzles you.

28 THURSDAY
Moon Age Day 8   Moon Sign Capricorn

Love and leisure should be equally important to most Geminis at the moment. Everything comes together today to make for a contented and happy interlude and one that doesn't depend on being out there fighting for money. You really can discover today that the best things in life are free and a great contentment should follow.

29 FRIDAY
Moon Age Day 9   Moon Sign Capricorn

This is likely to be a great time for broadening your intellectual horizons. What really stands out at the moment is your overriding desire for freedom and a need to express yourself fully, especially when you are in company. Your response to the ideas of others at work is likely to be guarded, mainly because you think you know better.

30 SATURDAY   *Moon Age Day 10   Moon Sign Capricorn*

This would be an excellent period for travelling, for making visits of one sort or another and for building new business and social connections. People find you good to know and you should be happiest when your many gifts are fully on display. It's time to preen yourself a little and even to feel slightly proud of your achievements.

♊

October

2017

1 SUNDAY
Moon Age Day 11   Moon Sign Aquarius

You can get closer to some of your goals at the moment using a combination of sound common sense and raw intuition. This is a strange concoction and one that anyone other than another Gemini might find difficult to understand. Energy levels remain generally high and there isn't much you would shy away from now.

2 MONDAY
Moon Age Day 12   Moon Sign Aquarius

Though there is little doubt your ego is strong at the moment, you retain your usual ability to turn on the charm whenever necessary. This is fortunate because you need to let those around you know how much you care about them and also reassure family members of your continued practical and emotional support.

3 TUESDAY
Moon Age Day 13   Moon Sign Pisces

Certain ambitious projects will have to be put on hold in favour of simply doing what you expect of yourself and what others are anxious for you to do. Your sense of fulfilment is closely tied to personal attachments at the present time and your ego can be slightly dented if someone very important to you lets you down.

4 WEDNESDAY
Moon Age Day 14   Moon Sign Pisces

There is just a slight possibility that you will be allowing hunches to gain the upper hand and as a result you could be involving yourself in something that is just a little dodgy. You really do need to know what you are doing at the present time because although success is never far from you, scrupulous honesty is essential.

5 THURSDAY
Moon Age Day 15   Moon Sign Aries

Although you need to pace yourself it should be fairly easy to get through more or less everything that is really important today. At the same time your social impulses are beginning to grow and you won't be at all content if you are expected to keep your head down all the time. Mixing with others is crucial.

6 FRIDAY
Moon Age Day 16   Moon Sign Aries

You have great sympathy at the moment for anyone who is having problems or who cannot deal with situations without becoming deeply anxious. Not only are you likely to offer advice but you also have what it takes to assume command and to sort things out. This ability gets you noticed and means you will have the support you need later.

7 SATURDAY
Moon Age Day 17   Moon Sign Taurus

You could be slightly vulnerable to the coercive tactics of people who are dishonest. Keep your ears and eyes open and turn your intuition up to full when it comes to assessing those around you. Not everyone has your best interests at heart so be sure to keep your wits about you.

8 SUNDAY
Moon Age Day 18   Moon Sign Taurus

There is plenty of reason to be out of bed early today and getting on quickly with all jobs that need to be done as a matter of routine. This will allow you more hours later to do whatever takes your fancy. This would be a good day for travel and for getting out and about generally. You feel the need to see new faces and places.

9 MONDAY
Moon Age Day 19   Moon Sign Taurus

You may be becoming slightly anxious about something but you can alleviate this tendency by sharing your worries with others. Someone in your vicinity will most likely be happy to listen to what you have to say and will offer the best sort of advice. You are also presently very supportive of younger or vulnerable family members.

10 TUESDAY   *Moon Age Day 20   Moon Sign Gemini*

You can share interesting ideas with others today but when it comes to getting things done you would be better off relying on your own initiative. This is because those around you, no matter how willing they may be, will not arrange things the way you want and probably don't have your staying power either.

11 WEDNESDAY   *Moon Age Day 21   Moon Sign Gemini*

The lunar high brings with it the necessary breeze of change that can blow away some of the recent difficulties. You will be determined, happy to go that extra mile and also willing to do whatever proves to be necessary in terms of changing old or outmoded routines. Get to grips with your finances today.

12 THURSDAY   *Moon Age Day 22   Moon Sign Cancer*

Because life can be fairly chaotic at present it might seem as though you are avoiding some of your responsibilities. Even if you don't actually have enough time to get everything done you need to reassure those around you that it is your intention to get round to all your duties as soon as it becomes possible.

13 FRIDAY   *Moon Age Day 23   Moon Sign Cancer*

You can't afford to trust to luck as much as you sometimes would and need to check and re-check details whenever possible. Today should bring you slightly closer to your heart's desire in a personal sense and can offer much in the way of social diversion. What it won't do is to make you a great deal better off financially.

14 SATURDAY   *Moon Age Day 24   Moon Sign Leo*

Your normal daily routines can now be interrupted by various small mishaps, meaning that some tasks have to be undertaken again. Don't give in to doubts or worries that are not based in reality and do your best to remain optimistic. This might not be easy but at least life is interesting and, on occasions, very funny.

15 SUNDAY
Moon Age Day 25   Moon Sign Leo

Activities that take place behind closed doors are your stock in trade for the moment because you are not as keen to get out and about as much as is usually the case for Gemini. Chances are that you will be fairly content with your own company and that you won't be seeking too much in the way of society.

16 MONDAY
Moon Age Day 26   Moon Sign Virgo

Co-operation is needed on a grand scale today if you are not to allow your ego to get in the way. What with one planet and another it is now as big as a bus and that can spell a few problems when you come up against similar types. On the other hand, the more modest you show yourself to be today, the greater will be the rewards.

17 TUESDAY
Moon Age Day 27   Moon Sign Virgo

Today is good for work-related matters and for setting things straight where any confusion has started to creep in. You have what it takes to increase your general popularity and may also be feeling quite romantic. Do something for your lover that they don't expect and whilst you are at it think up a unique gift.

18 WEDNESDAY
Moon Age Day 28   Moon Sign Libra

You could be working harder and harder on the treadmill of life, or at least that's the way it seems just at present. Actually things are going rather better than you might think so don't ignore a slight tendency on your part to be pessimistic today. Within just a few hours you should be right back on form.

19 THURSDAY
Moon Age Day 29   Moon Sign Libra

For much of the time today you will be getting down to brass tacks in both your professional and personal life. Seeing things the way they really are isn't difficult for you at present and there are very few shades of grey about. This is in sharp contrast to people with whom you are mixing and the result could be a little aggravation.

20 FRIDAY
Moon Age Day 0   Moon Sign Libra

This is a socially helpful period and it seems as though Gemini is steadying down a little – at least with regard to those issues you see as being of primary importance. You will still be quite definite in your opinions. It's just that you will not force them down the throats of other people to quite the same extent now.

21 SATURDAY
Moon Age Day 1   Moon Sign Scorpio

Group encounters and the rewards that come from friendship turn out to be the most significant factors this Saturday. It is unlikely you will be pushing yourself too hard, if at all, if you are at work. What appeals to you most right now is the opportunity to get out and about and to have fun in good company.

22 SUNDAY
Moon Age Day 2   Moon Sign Scorpio

What really sets you apart at the moment is how funny you tend to be. Others are closely monitoring the things you say and do and you show a positive face to the world. This is Gemini at its best and there is no doubt about your sincerity and your ability to work hard for the world in general. Along comes your social conscience.

23 MONDAY
Moon Age Day 3   Moon Sign Sagittarius

Personal and intimate matters bring out the best in you today and it's just as well they do because getting anything concrete done whilst the lunar low is around could be rather difficult. Take time out to show your lover just how important they are to you. Buy a small gift or do something unexpected in order to drive away your own blues.

24 TUESDAY
Moon Age Day 4   Moon Sign Sagittarius

You are still not on form in a practical sense and some of your dreams and ambitions might seem to be either in tatters or at the very least becoming less likely by the moment. That's simply because you are showing the pessimistic side of your nature. Don't do anything but simply watch and wait. Drastic action now would be a mistake.

25 WEDNESDAY   *Moon Age Day 5   Moon Sign Sagittarius*

You will feel your best rewards today when you are associated with others. Across the last month or so there have been times when other individuals have really got on your nerves but now you are much more patient and tend to take little reversals in your stride. Creative pursuits may prove to be part of what makes the midweek period fun.

26 THURSDAY   *Moon Age Day 6   Moon Sign Capricorn*

Don't be surprised to discover that you are really busy today. It will seem as if everything you have to do comes due in the same few hours, and other people will constantly be calling upon your assistance and expertise. Ingenuity will be present in cartloads when you need it the most and you won't easily run out of steam.

27 FRIDAY   *Moon Age Day 7   Moon Sign Capricorn*

You should join a new group or get involved in some new team activity – for no other reason than your own enjoyment. Not everything you do has to have a practical side or a financial reward. On the contrary your greatest pleasure at the moment is likely to come free of charge. Keep in touch with people who live abroad or at a distance.

28 SATURDAY   *Moon Age Day 8   Moon Sign Aquarius*

You will want to be active on the social scene, even if you feel quite withdrawn in some ways. It's likely that you will be playing the prima donna but this period is excellent for your love life and others find you immensely attractive. Your outgoing and happy-go-lucky nature is likely to appeal to just about everyone at present.

29 SUNDAY   *Moon Age Day 9   Moon Sign Aquarius*

Your general sense of satisfaction with your own efforts is likely to be on the increase and you take a broad-minded approach to many situations. This is especially true with regard to family members, some of whom are behaving in a way that you wouldn't have countenanced before. Maybe you are simply growing older and wiser?

30 MONDAY
Moon Age Day 10   Moon Sign Pisces

At the start of a new working week you may well find that travel and all intellectual pursuits appeal to you. It might be hard to concentrate on mundane matters when your mind is wandering so much but you do show yourself to be interesting to know. This alone means others notice you more and will do all they can to lend you a hand.

31 TUESDAY
Moon Age Day 11   Moon Sign Pisces

New work initiatives are the name of the game for Gemini now and even if you can only make little changes you will be happier than leaving everything the way it is. Resist the insatiable urge to tamper with things that are running perfectly well or you risk creating problems where there were previously none.

November

2017

1 WEDNESDAY
Moon Age Day 12   Moon Sign Pisces

Any chance to strike up some form of new social contract should be grasped with both hands. This is most certainly the case when you are dealing with unconventional types, many of whom seem to be especially attractive to you at this time. Have fun when you are away from work and socialise as much as possible through November.

2 THURSDAY
Moon Age Day 13   Moon Sign Aries

You can get the best of both worlds today when it comes to work and home and it should also be quite possible for you to mix business with pleasure in a very successful way. It appears that Gemini is truly on form at this time and you will be especially good when it comes to getting your ideas and opinions across to all sorts of people.

3 FRIDAY
Moon Age Day 14   Moon Sign Aries

Routine events come and go and you may discover that you get a great deal done while mentally on automatic pilot. Your mind will often be elsewhere and there is a sort of dreamy quality to your nature that others find distinctly appealing. Don't be at all surprised if you find that you are rapidly becoming someone's romantic ideal.

4 SATURDAY
Moon Age Day 15   Moon Sign Taurus

People seem to be especially demanding today and much of your time will be given over to sorting them out in one way or another. This trend is so evident that it might be quite difficult to get anything much done for yourself – which could lead to some frustration. In a social sense you are now likely to ring the changes regularly.

5 SUNDAY
Moon Age Day 16   Moon Sign Taurus

You continue to be one of the main attractions in your social circle and once again find the means to mix business with pleasure in a very useful and enjoyable way. Take over some of the organisation if you want things to go seamlessly, otherwise you could discover that details are either forgotten or mishandled.

6 MONDAY
Moon Age Day 17   Moon Sign Gemini

Pushing ahead and getting what you want from life are simply two of your talents right now. Energy is definitely on the increase and you seem to be especially active at work or in terms of your major responsibilities. There are gains to be made by simply being in the right place at the right time and you have a great desire to prosper.

7 TUESDAY
Moon Age Day 18   Moon Sign Gemini

With the lunar high comes a definite sense of drive and enthusiasm. You shouldn't find it at all hard to ring the changes and you will be much more likely now to spend time away from home. Despite these facts, and the lunar high, you may feel happier if someone you know well is close at hand and if you can truly share with them.

8 WEDNESDAY
Moon Age Day 19   Moon Sign Cancer

People seem quite determined to do you favours today. This could be because you are smiling so much and putting yourself out on their behalf without even realising the fact. Some simple good luck could help you in meetings and discussions and potentially lead to significant achievement.

9 THURSDAY
Moon Age Day 20   Moon Sign Cancer

Things mechanical could be giving you one or two problems right now and it might be best to leave their repair to people who know what they are doing. Typical Gemini tampering might only make matters worse, though it is just possible that you will learn something on the way. Friends could find you slightly frustrating today.

10 FRIDAY
Moon Age Day 21   Moon Sign Leo

It's time to put yourself in the limelight and to work towards a weekend that can be very special to you and those you love. Gemini is likely to be quite romantic at present and it looks as though you can make the best of impressions on someone who is truly important to you. Stand by to meet Gemini the lover – an inspiring sight.

11 SATURDAY
Moon Age Day 22   Moon Sign Leo

Today should be an especially helpful day in terms of communication. Getting the message across to others ought to prove very easy and you won't want to miss a single opportunity to tell it how it is. Some practical jobs could be a chore, but not if you get them out of the way very early in the day.

12 SUNDAY
Moon Age Day 23   Moon Sign Virgo

You are still likely to be on fine form and quite willing to do whatever is necessary to make the sort of impression for which your zodiac sign is famous. People like you for your dynamism, your sense of humour and your easy-going attitude, all of which are present in great measure. Don't expect too much financial support for the moment.

13 MONDAY
Moon Age Day 24   Moon Sign Virgo

Look to your finances and the many ways you can think about improving them in the days and weeks ahead. It could be that there is slightly more money around than you might have expected or it is possible that you are simply being much more careful in the way you use cash than you have been. You might tend to make and keep lists just now.

14 TUESDAY
Moon Age Day 25   Moon Sign Libra

This is one of the best days of the month during which to get new projects off the ground and you will have plenty of know-how when it matters the most. Not that you are capable of doing absolutely everything. There will be moments when it would be best to call in the support of an expert – even though you may resent doing so.

15 WEDNESDAY · Moon Age Day 26 · Moon Sign Libra

With a great desire to assert your opinions and to have your say no matter what, you could fall foul of someone who has very different ideas. It would be far better at the moment to agree with people rather than to argue with them. All the same, you won't be crossed and will cut off your nose to spite your face under certain circumstances.

16 THURSDAY · Moon Age Day 27 · Moon Sign Libra

Great co-operation is needed today if you want to avoid getting yourself into pointless arguments. The opinions of other people could really get your goat at the moment, though for no apparent reason but your own present mood. Some restrictions may be placed on you at work and that could be why you are somewhat out of sorts.

17 FRIDAY · Moon Age Day 28 · Moon Sign Scorpio

Keep up the speed at which you are living your life, at least for today. Make sure that as many things as possible are achieved in this period just ahead of the lunar low and enjoy the appreciation that comes your way when you do something relatively small for those around you. Family issues are likely to be on your mind at this time.

18 SATURDAY · Moon Age Day 0 · Moon Sign Scorpio

There are minor setbacks and changes of pace that have to be dealt with today. As a result life may feel jerky and lack any real continuity. As the hours pass you will become a little more satisfied with your lot but even by the end of the day you could be inclined to snap at people or to withdraw from things you don't like.

19 SUNDAY · Moon Age Day 1 · Moon Sign Sagittarius

Whilst it is clear that you are presently eager for success, you might have to work that much harder to achieve it. Although not really a stumbling block to you, it is just possible that you may look with envy at certain individuals who seem to come up smelling of roses, no matter how little effort they put in.

20 MONDAY
Moon Age Day 2 Moon Sign Sagittarius

The lunar low is still around and you continue to have to work that much harder to achieve your objectives. As ever, it would be more sensible to simply put things on hold for a day or two – but you may remain quite adamant about your own opinions and refuse to let anyone tell you that you are wrong. Keep up your efforts to make changes at home.

21 TUESDAY
Moon Age Day 3 Moon Sign Sagittarius

Some professional advantages look likely today and these may come via the good offices of other people. You may be able to make some good contacts with people who could be useful to you, a fact that is as evident in your social life as it will be at work. There may still be a little conflict in your personal life but it can be curbed today.

22 WEDNESDAY
Moon Age Day 4 Moon Sign Capricorn

As always you are willing to go to great lengths to be both noticed and appreciated but you could easily become upset if you feel you are not receiving the attention that is due to you. If you can't get what you want by one means you are likely to try another and then another. All in all it would be easier to relax a little.

23 THURSDAY
Moon Age Day 5 Moon Sign Capricorn

There could be the odd pitfall to watch out for when it comes to your money today. Perhaps you are not quite as sure of certain details as you might be? It's time to check and then check again in order to make sure that all the figures add up. Socially, you will be pleased to mix with people who are different from your usual circle.

24 FRIDAY
Moon Age Day 6 Moon Sign Aquarius

Don't allow your pride to get in the way of good communications with others today. Even though it might hurt to admit the fact, someone might know better than you do and you will only make matters worse by refusing to accept this. Creative pursuits work well today – maybe sorting out all those Christmas decorations?

25 SATURDAY   *Moon Age Day 7   Moon Sign Aquarius*

You now put your views across with great conviction and won't be easily dissuaded from doing those things you see as being necessary. There is no tendency to avoid hard work and you will expect everyone around you to keep up. Do try to show a little consideration for individuals who are not as energetic as you are.

26 SUNDAY   *Moon Age Day 8   Moon Sign Aquarius*

Travel is now positively highlighted and this particular Sunday goes better for you if you get as much change into your life as you can. Drop the responsibilities for a while and find ways to please both yourself and your lover. If you are between romantic partners now is definitely the time to keep your eyes open.

27 MONDAY   *Moon Age Day 9   Moon Sign Pisces*

There is a strong desire to be number one today, no matter what you are doing. This is going to be around for a while and you need to find ways to get what you want, though without ruffling feathers on the way. Don't be afraid to take the odd gamble and push yourself physically whilst your energy levels are high.

28 TUESDAY   *Moon Age Day 10   Moon Sign Pisces*

Your personal impact on the world remains generally strong. You have what it takes to move mountains at the moment, though you could be looking at a few that would be better off left exactly where they are. Focus your attention on those matters you have the ability to alter because it is quantity that matters now and not quality.

29 WEDNESDAY   *Moon Age Day 11   Moon Sign Aries*

Today you are likely to come face to face with people who have very different ideas and ambitions than you have. Being cast in an opposing role is part of what the planets are about just now but that doesn't mean you have to react harshly. Disagreement doesn't necessarily mean disagreeableness. Show how kind you can be.

30 THURSDAY *Moon Age Day 12   Moon Sign Aries*

At present you have an insatiable appetite for new experiences, impressions and situations. You will be especially responsive to others and may well be making new friends around this time. With Christmas now in view the social whirl is likely to be beginning. As usual you take the lead in helping everyone have a really good time.

Ⅱ
December
2017

1 FRIDAY
Moon Age Day 13   Moon Sign Taurus

This is a day when you can be the life and soul of the party – that is if there is one happening today. There is a strong boost to your romantic potential and you want to be out there enjoying yourself. It looks as though the Christmas spirit is going to come early this year – at least as far as Gemini is concerned.

2 SATURDAY
Moon Age Day 14   Moon Sign Taurus

You now enter a period of hard work, even though in some situations you are putting in more effort than is strictly necessary. At least by doing things the hard way you can be certain that they are done properly, and that is what seems to matter the most to you now. Routines should prove to be comfortable rather than irritating at present.

3 SUNDAY
☿ *Moon Age Day 15   Moon Sign Gemini*

Mental and physical strengths are evident and for the next two days you should be able to achieve things that you failed to address earlier. It seems as though you have boundless energy and that you are filled with enthusiasm as a natural consequence of being a Gemini. Use these trends, don't analyse them.

4 MONDAY
☿ *Moon Age Day 16   Moon Sign Gemini*

Where important objectives are concerned you should not be afraid to take the odd chance. That doesn't mean putting yourself in any sort of danger but rather striking while the iron is hot when it comes to controlling your own life. From a financial point of view you could discover you are better off than you previously thought.

5 TUESDAY ☿ *Moon Age Day 17 Moon Sign Cancer*

Your mind works overtime now and you have an insatiable curiosity about a thousand different things. Keep up with correspondence and don't forget all those Christmas cards you probably haven't even bought yet. It's a busy life and you may have to compartmentalise the day in order to get everything done.

6 WEDNESDAY ☿ *Moon Age Day 18 Moon Sign Cancer*

Today you use your strong independent streak to broaden your horizons. Closer to the end of the month you will find any real progress difficult to make, not because of planetary influences but on account of Christmas. That's why it is so important to push ahead at the moment and make a real display of your talents.

7 THURSDAY ☿ *Moon Age Day 19 Moon Sign Leo*

This may be one of the best days of the month to initiate new projects and to get life moving at a fairly heady pace. People who have real influence are able to help you out but before they can it will be necessary for you to ask for assistance. People from the past are likely to be coming into your mind but that is normal for December.

8 FRIDAY ☿ *Moon Age Day 20 Moon Sign Leo*

Friendships continue to be a source of reward in your life at the moment and today should see newcomers on the horizon. Maybe you will meet these people because of Christmas social obligations or it could be that you will come across them in the course of your working life. Wherever they appear, take notice.

9 SATURDAY ☿ *Moon Age Day 21 Moon Sign Virgo*

Travel and conversations are positively highlighted today and you will mix quite freely with all manner of people on your journey through Saturday. This would be a good time for shopping, though probably not on your own. Friends are great to have around when there are bargains to be sought and you can have a chat too!

10 SUNDAY ☿ *Moon Age Day 22   Moon Sign Virgo*

Your affable Gemini charm makes everyone around you keen to know you better and your popularity is as high as it often is. Whether you are satisfied with your own efforts at the moment remains to be seen. In some ways this could be one of those days during which little things constantly delay you and hamper your efforts.

11 MONDAY ☿ *Moon Age Day 23   Moon Sign Virgo*

Today you show yourself to have a brilliant, imaginative mind. It is possible to make intuitive leaps and to be well ahead of the game in most situations. On the other hand it is possible that you will be rather outspoken and you might cause a little upset by refusing to accept that other people sometimes know better than you do.

12 TUESDAY ☿ *Moon Age Day 24   Moon Sign Libra*

Making a big impact on the world remains fairly easy, even if you tend to upset one or two people on the way. You will still be fairly outspoken and unwilling to compromise on those occasions when you are certain of your ground. Your personality is especially potent around now.

13 WEDNESDAY ☿ *Moon Age Day 25   Moon Sign Libra*

There are some fairly wild ideas about today and some of these could cloud your common sense. Nevertheless you are likely to be having a good time and even if you only achieve one tenth of what you would wish, you should be getting on fairly well. In relationships there is likely to be a more contented phase on the way.

14 THURSDAY ☿ *Moon Age Day 26   Moon Sign Scorpio*

You can now break from usual routines and improve your life in a positive way. Self-awareness and a solid resolve are the weapons you need to get ahead, together with a silver tongue and an enchanting manner. There are fewer adversaries about now, maybe because you see the world as your friend and not your opponent.

15 FRIDAY ☿ *Moon Age Day 27 Moon Sign Scorpio*

Your response to many of today's events is in keeping with the overall characteristics of Gemini. Your actions and decisions may make a big impact on the world and you shouldn't have any trouble at all bringing other people round to your point of view, no matter how radical or unusual it may be.

16 SATURDAY ☿ *Moon Age Day 28 Moon Sign Scorpio*

This would be an especially pleasant day for social encounters and for making the running when it comes to acting alongside groups of people. Short trips and positive chats with almost anyone are also indicated. You might not seem to get a great deal done in a practical sense but you are very good at networking.

17 SUNDAY ☿ *Moon Age Day 29 Moon Sign Sagittarius*

If it seems as if everyone else is getting ahead much better and faster than you are, it is the lunar low that should take the blame. Actually it may not be too potent this time around and it does at least give you more time away from the social spotlight to think about all those jobs that are still to be done but which you haven't addressed yet.

18 MONDAY ☿ *Moon Age Day 0 Moon Sign Sagittarius*

To compensate for the Moon being in your opposite sign, your chart shows some redeeming planetary influences, which could make you more vocal than would normally be the case whilst the lunar low is around. You may also be alert and discriminating, though it might be better not to make too many long-term decisions until tomorrow.

19 TUESDAY ☿ *Moon Age Day 1 Moon Sign Capricorn*

You have a wonderful diplomatic talent and a great sense of style at the moment. Socially speaking you should be right in your element because with all that is happening around you there is a chance for you to shine at every turn. This may not be your favourite time of year but you are really getting into the swing of things.

20 WEDNESDAY ☿ *Moon Age Day 2   Moon Sign Capricorn*

This is a good day for family dealings of any sort and at last you may be ready for all that the festive season is likely to bring. If you have been outspoken about anything in the past you can now put matters right once and for all, and the entertaining element of today is enhanced by your own willingness to 'act the part'.

21 THURSDAY   ☿ *Moon Age Day 3   Moon Sign Capricorn*

There are some mental challenges about at the moment and you won't shy away from a single one of them. You like to win, no matter what you are doing and you would be right in your element with any sporting activities. Try to avoid loading yourself down with too much responsibility because there are also good times to be had.

22 FRIDAY   ☿ *Moon Age Day 4   Moon Sign Aquarius*

Suddenly you are almost manic in your desire to convince others that your point of view is the only one that is right or relevant. In your clearer moments you will realise that this is not actually the case but for now woe betide anyone who disagrees. The best adage to remember today would be live and let live.

23 SATURDAY   *Moon Age Day 5   Moon Sign Aquarius*

You need to be both socially and romantically active today if you want to get the very best out of what present trends are offering. There is no point at all in sitting in a corner and waiting for life to come to you. On the contrary you should promote good times rather than reacting to them and with plenty of ideas in your head – it's easy.

24 SUNDAY   *Moon Age Day 6   Moon Sign Pisces*

A new idea or pursuit should prove to be quite inspirational today – not that you will have much time to think about it. It is towards the enjoyment of others that your mind tends to turn on Christmas Eve and there isn't much doubt that you get a great deal of enjoyment yourself from your efforts to make the whole world smile.

25 MONDAY
Moon Age Day 7   Moon Sign Pisces

Christmas Day allows you to brush up your appearance and to appear at your absolute best, no matter what company you happen to be keeping. It will be easy to get into the swing of the day and you find ways and means to accommodate everyone. Things definitely work out best when you are in charge and when others know it.

26 TUESDAY
Moon Age Day 8   Moon Sign Pisces

It is time to encourage your love life and Boxing Day offers the best chance of romance across the entire Christmas period. Perhaps this is because you have more hours to concentrate on such matters or simply because you are in the right place at the right time. Friendships are also strengthened under present planetary trends.

27 WEDNESDAY
Moon Age Day 9   Moon Sign Aries

A certain acquisitive streak appears today, which is heightened by some of the gifts that are coming your way right now. Avoid a tendency for impulse buying in the sales, at least until you are sure that you need whatever is on offer. You might have to tactfully decline a particular offer around now.

28 THURSDAY
Moon Age Day 10   Moon Sign Aries

You could be rather too emotional for your own good at present and it would be better not to allow yourself to wallow in the past more than is strictly necessary. Perhaps divert your attention with a board game, or else travel a short distance to somewhere that you find particularly interesting. This is not a good day to spend too much time alone.

29 FRIDAY
Moon Age Day 11   Moon Sign Taurus

On the whole this is likely to prove a busy time at home, though you are also much in demand out there in the wider world and could well be travelling somewhere today. Try to avoid waste right now and find ways to use up all those odd scraps that are left over from the festivities. At the very least give it all to the birds.

30 SATURDAY   *Moon Age Day 12   Moon Sign Taurus*

Expect success on most fronts, although be aware that you may not be able to get things moving quite as quickly as you might wish given the time of year. It looks as though you will be taking a dynamic role in romantic matters and you are also extremely creative at the moment. Changes in and around your home are quite possible.

31 SUNDAY   *Moon Age Day 13   Moon Sign Gemini*

The good times continue and the lunar high on New Year's Eve offers you new incentives as well as an opportunity to correct something from the past. There is a chance of advancement about now, though this may be slightly eclipsed by the time of year and tonight's festivities. Put in that extra bit of effort to impress someone.

RISING SIGNS FOR GEMINI

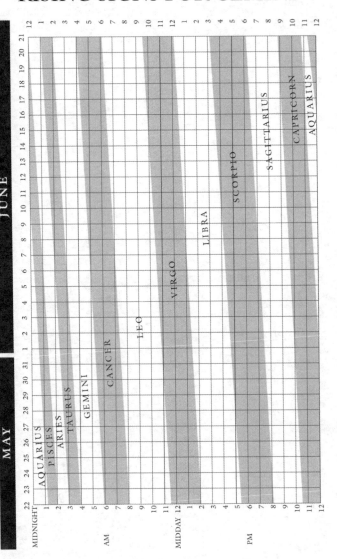

THE ZODIAC, PLANETS AND CORRESPONDENCES

The Earth revolves around the Sun once every calendar year, so when viewed from Earth the Sun appears in a different part of the sky as the year progresses. In astrology, these parts of the sky are divided into the signs of the zodiac and this means that the signs are organised in a circle. The circle begins with Aries and ends with Pisces.

Taking the zodiac sign as a starting point, astrologers then work with all the positions of planets, stars and many other factors to calculate horoscopes and birth charts and tell us what the stars have in store for us.

The table below shows the planets and Elements for each of the signs of the zodiac. Each sign belongs to one of the four Elements: Fire, Air, Earth or Water. Fire signs are creative and enthusiastic; Air signs are mentally active and thoughtful; Earth signs are constructive and practical; Water signs are emotional and have strong feelings.

It also shows the metals and gemstones associated with, or corresponding with, each sign. The correspondence is made when a metal or stone possesses properties that are held in common with a particular sign of the zodiac.

Finally, the table shows the opposite of each star sign – this is the opposite sign in the astrological circle.

Placed	Sign	Symbol	Element	Planet	Metal	Stone	Opposite
1	Aries	Ram	Fire	Mars	Iron	Bloodstone	Libra
2	Taurus	Bull	Earth	Venus	Copper	Sapphire	Scorpio
3	Gemini	Twins	Air	Mercury	Mercury	Tiger's Eye	Sagittarius
4	Cancer	Crab	Water	Moon	Silver	Pearl	Capricorn
5	Leo	Lion	Fire	Sun	Gold	Ruby	Aquarius
6	Virgo	Maiden	Earth	Mercury	Mercury	Sardonyx	Pisces
7	Libra	Scales	Air	Venus	Copper	Sapphire	Aries
8	Scorpio	Scorpion	Water	Pluto	Plutonium	Jasper	Taurus
9	Sagittarius	Archer	Fire	Jupiter	Tin	Topaz	Gemini
10	Capricorn	Goat	Earth	Saturn	Lead	Black Onyx	Cancer
11	Aquarius	Waterbearer	Air	Uranus	Uranium	Amethyst	Leo
12	Pisces	Fishes	Water	Neptune	Tin	Moonstone	Virgo